Accountancy in Transition

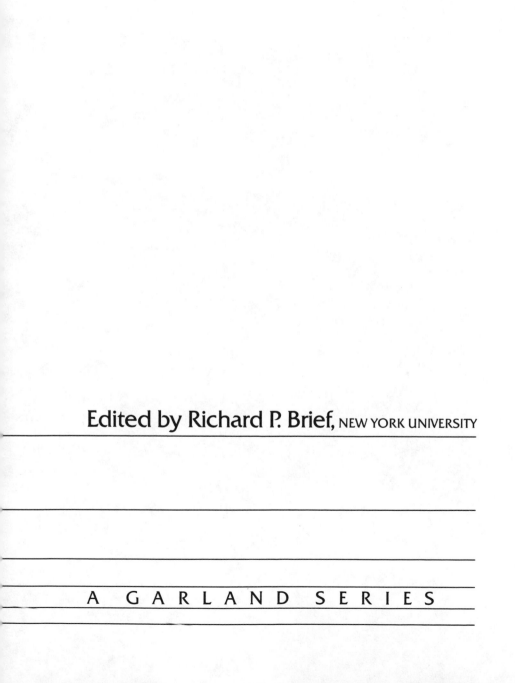

Edited by Richard P. Brief, NEW YORK UNIVERSITY

A GARLAND SERIES

Further Essays on
the History of Accounting

Basil S. Yamey

Garland Publishing, Inc.
New York & London   1982

ACKNOWLEDGMENTS

"Some Reflections on the Writing of a General History of Accounting," "Early Views on the Origins and Development of Bookkeeping and Accounting," "Oldcastle, Peele and Mellis, a Case of Plagiarism in the Sixteenth Century," "Two Seventeenth Century Accounting 'Statements'," and "George Peacock, an Early 'Translator' of Pacioli" are reprinted by permission of *Accounting and Business Research.*

"Accounting in the Middle Ages, 500 to 1500" was first published in the Dictionary of the Middle Ages, Volume I, Joseph R. Strayer, Editor-in-Chief. Copyright © 1982 by the American Council of Learned Societies (New York: Charles Scribner's Sons, 1982) and is here reprinted by permission of Charles Scribner's Sons.

"Peele's Two Treatises in Context" is reprinted by permission of Daigakudo Books Co.

"Compound Journal Entries in Early Treatises on Bookkeeping," and "The Index to the Ledger: Some Historical Notes" are reprinted by permission of *The Accounting Review.*

"The 'Partimenti' Account: A Discarded Practice" is reprinted by permission of *Abacus*

"The Typographical Ambiguities in Pacioli's 'Summa': Further Notes" is reprinted by permission of the Gutenberg-Gesellschaft.

Library of Congress Cataloging in Publication Data

Yamey, Basil S.
　Further essays on the history of accounting.

　(Accountancy in transition)
　Reprint of works originally published 1979–1982.
　　1. Accounting—History—Addresses, essays, lectures.
I. Title.　II. Series.
HF5605.Y363　1982　　657'.09　　82-82491
ISBN 0-8240-5339-7

The volumes in this series are printed on acid-free, 250-year-life paper.

Printed in the United States of America

Preface

The twelve papers reprinted in this book were written between 1977 and 1981, and follow on my earlier papers which were collected in *Essays on the History of Accounting* (Arno Press, New York, 1978).

The first three papers cover broad subjects. The first presents a discussion and assessment of the problems and difficulties which confront anyone bold enough to embark on writing a general history of accounting. While it lays stress on prevailing obstacles and highlights lacunae, it is, I believe, also more positive, for instance in indicating interesting terrain awaiting its explorers. The second paper is an attempt partly to fill one of the gaps, the development of accounting in the Middle Ages in Europe. It is based largely on secondary source material, much of which has not been used by historians of accounting. The third paper collects and comments upon early views (up to about 1860) published on the beginnings and development of bookkeeping and accounts.

The next two papers are concerned primarily with the works of James Peele, by far the most interesting of the sixteenth-century English writers on merchants' accounts. The longer of the two papers places Peele's contributions in context; and, in so doing, it analyses all published treatises on accounts up to 1569, concentrating on selected aspects. The shorter paper examines John Mellis's book of 1588 as the product of its compiler's proclivities as plagiarist, notably of Peele's two books. It shows, I believe conclusively, that contrary to the views of Fabio Besta and others, the Mellis book is of no value at all as evidence for the proposition that Luca Pacioli based his tractate on the double-entry system upon some earlier manuscript exposition.

The remaining papers cover a variety of more limited topics, each indicated sufficiently by its title.

The paper on accounting in the Middle Ages is a slightly modified version of the article written for the *Dictionary of the Middle Ages*. The main difference between the two versions is the inclusion of an additional paragraph on page 16, and an additional sentence in one or two places. The list of references is somewhat more extensive here. I take the opportunity of this reprinting of the paper to thank those who gave me valuable guidance in what for me was unfamiliar territory: F.R.H. du Boulay, J. Gillingham, P.D.A. Harvey, R. C. Hoffmann and D. P. Waley; and also to acknowledge the useful suggestions made by the editorial staff of the *Dictionary*.

I am grateful to the editors and publishers who have so willingly authorised me to reprint papers which had first appeared in their publication.

Last but by no means least, I want to thank Margaret Kosowicz, my secretary, for all her help—and patience—in the preparation of this volume.

Basil S. Yamey
April, 1982

Contents

"Two Typographical Ambiguities in Pacioli's 'Summa': Further Notes," *Gutenberg-Jahrbuch*, 1980.

Addenda

SOME REFLECTIONS ON THE
WRITING OF A GENERAL
HISTORY OF ACCOUNTING

Some Reflections on the Writing of a General History of Accounting[*]

B. S. Yamey

Introduction

A character in a recent novel (*The Middle Ground*, by Margaret Drabble) laments:

> Everything has too much history. No wonder a pattern is slow to emerge from such a thick clutter of cross references, from such trivia, from such serious but hidden connections...

Accounting, also, has a lot of history. Its annals begin, we are told, with the birth of writing. Each additional year adds to the volume of records; and, at the other end of the time scale, new archaeological excavations sometimes do the same.[1]

Moreover, and evidently even more unmanageable for the historian, there is evidence of accounting activity without written records, in pre-literate or non-literate societies. According to a respectable theory, mathematical calculations of considerable complexity must have been executed in some pre-literate societies in order for people to have been able to set up megalithic constructions used for astronomical observation. Such societies would rather easily have coped with accounting processes and calculations. The composition and early performances of the poems of Homer also suggest the formidable powers of memory manifested before people could write. A much more recent example is that of the Ashanti Kingdom in eighteenth century West Africa, with a system of official record-keeping without writing.[2] Not surprisingly, there is evidence also of traders and others who have conducted their affairs without benefit of written accounts—but

with the help of what can be recognised as accounting processes. An interesting example concerns certain Berber merchants in North Africa. Until recent times partners in trading businesses often were illiterate. 'All the records were stored in their heads', to use the words of an anthropologist (who goes on to quote one of his informants, a member of a partnership: 'We are brothers; but when we do the accounts, we are enemies').[3]

Pity, therefore, the poor historian, or would-be-historian, who is bold enough to embark upon writing a general history of accounting—pity him even if he, realistically, decides to ignore non-written accounting; and even if he decides to confine his efforts, arbitrarily, to Europe and North America (an arbitrary restriction which I, for one, would feel it imperative to impose upon myself).

The Bohemian banker and scholar, Karl Peter Kheil, a giant in our field, worked for 40 years on a universal history of bookkeeping and accounting. Shortly before his death early this century he wrote: 'One has to be content with fragments of, or contributions to, the history of bookkeeping, so long as the sources and the collected manuscripts and printed materials necessary for a general history of the science have not been fully researched, winnowed and tested'.[4] During the inter-war period the Dutch scholar, Pieter Kats, who was employed in the oil trade, tried hard to organise a team to write a general history of accounting. He enlisted the support of Dr. O. Bauer, a Russian who had written a book on the subject in 1911; and he evidently had Professor Henry Rand Hatfield nibbling at the bait. But nothing was to come of it. Hatfield wrote to Kats, in 1927, that he had been asked to write three books—a college textbook on accounting; a 'treatise on profits considered from the viewpoints of economics, law and accounting'; and the collaborative history of bookkeeping proposed by

---

[*]This is the substance of a lecture given at the Third International Congress of Accounting Historians, London, August 1980, under the title 'On *Not* Writing a General History of Accounting'. Some minor changes have been made for publication, and bibliographical references and footnotes added.

[1]For example, recent excavations have revealed a previously unknown kingdom ca. 2,400 BC, named Ebla, in Northern Syria. In 1974–75 the archives were uncovered, with many cuneiform tablets, several being described as bookkeeping records. P. Matthiae, *Ebla*, London, 1980.

[2]M. J. Herskovits, *Economic Anthropology*, revised ed., 1952, p. 420.

[3]J. Waterbury, *North for the Trade: The Life and Times of a Berber Merchant*, Berkeley, 1972, pp. 46–8.

[4]Quoted in B. Penndorf, *Geschichte der Buchhaltung in Deutschland*, Leipzig, 1913, preface.

Kats. Hatfield says the first would be most profitable, the second 'of more theoretical interest', and the third 'would fit in more with my own personal hobby'. But the last 'seems to imply a terrible amount of work'.[5] After having hovered indecisively among the three possibilities, he eventually decided not to write the history (nor, I believe, the book on profits)—a decision which has meant that we have been deprived of the fruits of Hatfield's immense knowledge of at least large tracts of the relevant material. (I suspect that one reason for Hatfield's decision was his striving after perfection, and his recognition that there was so much delving to be done before reasonably certain conclusions could be reached on even quite simple matters, such as the meaning of certain terms in Pacioli's treatise.)

Much good work has been done since the time of Kheil and the Kats and Hatfield discussions. And this is an occasion for acknowledging the major and remarkable contributions made by scholars who have died within recent years: A. C. Littleton, Raymond de Roover, Onko ten Have, J.-H. Vlaemminck, Ronald S. Edwards and Federigo Melis. Their works will figure prominently in any general history of accounting worthy of the name which comes to be written. But Hatfield's 'terrible amount of work' still remains to be done before the researching, winnowing and testing prescribed by Kheil have been carried far enough.

Gaps in the data, illustrated for the period 1500–1850

A general history of bookkeeping and accounting would be a worthwhile undertaking, even if it would inevitably have to present something of a bird's eye view. (I do not share Professor Elton's judgement that 'birds eye views are strictly for the birds').[6] But I foresee many difficulties. In the time at my disposal let me explore two quite different areas of difficulty. The first concerns, as it were, the data base now available to the historian. Here, rather than wander superficially over the centuries, I shall concentrate on the period roughly from 1500 to 1850, a period of major importance in economic history. (Incidentally, this period is sometimes described as a period of stagnation in accounting. If this description were apt, which I doubt, the very intriguing question would present itself: why did accounting remain

largely unchanged in a period which witnessed considerable economic change and growth?) The second concerns the significance of accounting, when my treatment will be even more episodic and illustrative, even briefer, but not confined to a particular historical period.

Bookkeeping and accounting are things done by people. Accounting records are human artefacts, created by people, to serve their purposes (or sometimes, perhaps, to give expression to a propensity to record and to calculate). I contend that, for several long periods and several important places, we have not collected, arranged and analysed enough of the facts about accounting methods and practices to get us far in the writing of reliable history.

Now the collection and study of facts are troublesome, labour-intensive, time-intensive, and often frustrating. And there is a tendency these days in several disciplines to give low status to this type of activity—which, however, is essential: we have to know pretty clearly what was done before we can come up with reasonably good answers as to why it was done, and what its consequences were.

Naturally, mere unearthing and collection of factual information is no more than the first step—but one at which, I confess, I have often found it pleasant to loiter. Francis Bacon dealt with it all in an interesting way in describing varieties of scientists. For him pure collectors—empiricists— were like ants. Philosophers in the realm of science were no better: they were like spiders who, with their logic, spun complex webs from their own bodies. The true scientists, for Bacon, were like bees, who extracted matter from flowers, and then refashioned it into honey, useful to all.[7] In the history of accounting we need many more bees, and even ants. And there have already been a few spiders, who, sitting in their armchairs (to change the metaphor) have been happy to deduce what must have happened in times past, and why it must have happened, by recourse to no more than knowledge of other events or developments that occurred more or less simultaneously, or, more perilously still, by drawing inferences from what was thought to be the spirit of the age, the *Zeitgeist*.

For England and Scotland for the period roughly 1500 to 1850, I believe that less than a score of sets of account-books kept by double entry have been examined systematically by his-

---

[5]Letter from H. R. Hatfield to P. Kats, 6 October, 1927. I am indebted to Professor S. Zeff for permission to quote from the Hatfield correspondence.
[6]G. R. Elton, *The Practice of History*, paperback edition, London, 1969, p. 94.

[7]See A. G. Debus, *Man and Nature in the Renaissance*, Cambridge, 1978, p. 104.

torians of accounting who have published their findings. To the best of my knowledge the number is far smaller for any other European country. And the tally is of the same order for records kept on other bases than double entry. In all, this is a fairly exiguous data base for the accounting historian. It is true, of course, that many other historians besides accounting historians have looked at accounting records and reported upon them. But useful, even indispensable, as much of their work has been from our specialised point of view, not infrequently historians with different specialised interests have not been well informed about accounting techniques, or have not been able to assess individual documents in terms of a complete system or of accounting processes.

Fortunately, the series of treatises on bookkeeping and accounts published from 1494 onwards provide some help in forming a view of early practices, especially of double-entry bookkeeping. They do enable one on occasions to understand more clearly the nature and purpose of particular procedures; and also to distinguish the more idiosyncratic from the more common form. But this source has to be used with discretion.

Moreover, the study of the treatises themselves has not been as thorough and complete as one would like it to be. The treatises published in the Netherlands have had especially admirable treatment, from de Waal and ten Have. The latter, however, went no further than 1800. Penndorf's analysis of the early German texts is exemplary— but he seems to have lost interest in works published after about 1650. The Italian treatises have been written about frequently, sometimes with scholarly care and insight, e.g. by Besta, Melis and Viganó. But some interesting early Italian authors have had no more than summary treatment, with early mistakes and misjudgements about them repeated without checking: for example, the contention that Venturi introduced what later came to be called *scrittura doppia a partite zoppe*, the limping double-entry system.[8] And we need a detailed scholarly analysis of Luca Pacioli's exposition of 1494—of the kind that has been accorded to the first printed work in almost any other branch of knowledge or arts—a task made easier in respect of Pacioli by Professor

Antinori's admirable work.[9] The French treatises call for more detailed study than they have had. And a step-by-step chronicle and analysis of the English treatises is a desideratum. Many of the early treatises in all languages were written by men with practical knowledge and experience, and much can be gleaned from their writings; and we may remind ourselves that those who only teach also sometimes know what goes on in the real world.

Precisely how and when did the practice of double entry spread from Italy to the rest of Europe (or to the rest of the world)? We know something, but not enough, about the dissemination of this technique, one still widely used six or seven centuries after its birth. (We have, of course, had well-documented accounts of the introduction of double entry into Japan). Again, how widespread was the use of double entry, say in England around 1700 or 1800? Or in Germany? As for England, in 1664 Thomas Mun, a merchant of London, wrote that a perfect merchant 'ought to be a good Penman, a good Arithmetician, and a good Accomptant, by that noble order of *Debtor* and *Creditor*, which is used only amongst Merchants'.[10] But did all or many Englishmen who qualified for the appellation 'merchant' know and use double entry? Richard Grassby, an historian who has studied a large number of extant merchants' records, has reported that 'genuine double-entry book-keeping was extremely rare in practice' in the seventeenth century.[11]

What about the United States? From the work of Alfred Chandler, the distinguished business historian, one would get the impression that early in the nineteenth century the double entry system was the standard system used in commerce and also by craftsmen, house builders, distillers and others.[12] William Baxter, however, found little of

---

[8]B. Venturi, *Della Scrittura Conteggiante di Possessioni*, Florence, 1655. The 'limping' system is one in which the cash account is not included in the ledger. Venturi has a cash account in the ledger in his system of double entry.

[9]I refer to Professor C. Antinori's accurate transcription of Pacioli's *Tractatus de computis et scripturis*, published in *Rivista Bancaria-Minerva Bancaria*, 1959, The numerous abbreviations in the original are printed in full in Antinori. As the original *Summa* is difficult to read, Antinori's transcription is invaluable. It replaces V. Gitti's less reliable work of 1878.

[10]T. Mun, *England's Treasure by Forraign Trade*, London, 1664.

[11]R. Grassby, 'The Rate of Profit in Seventeenth-Century England', *English Historical Review*, vol. 84, 1969, p. 748.

[12]A. D. Chandler, *The Visible Hand: The Managerial Revolution in American Business*, Cambridge, Mass., 1977, pp. 36 and 62.

double entry in colonial America.[13] Did the system spread so rapidly after Independence? And, if so, why? Clearly, a good deal remains to be done just to establish the facts.

The large number of books on bookkeeping and accounts which must have been bought in our period (1500–1850) may suggest that the double-entry system elucidated in them must have been widely used. But this would be a doubtful inference. Not everyone who today buys a cook book or recipe book becomes a good cook or uses the recipes. Many books on econometrics are bought by people who do not become econometricians. I suspect that knowledge of double entry was more widespread than its practice. We do not know how many merchants, manufacturers and their clerks had difficulties with the double entry system in practice. Sometimes it is clear from surviving account-books that they had difficulties: sometimes the system seems to have been introduced with good intentions, and then to have been allowed to lapse.[14] We know that teaching and textbooks often were tedious and mechanical, and possibly ineffective.[15] Edmond Degrange, senior, complained that students often spent as much as a year without getting a clear understanding of the system and its practical application. (He naturally claimed that his students,

using his method of study, were competent after a few weeks.[16]) A merchant of Rheims (in France), Jean Maillefert, around the middle of the seventeenth century expressed the view that as a subject of study bookkeeping by double entry demanded as much diligence and application as did philosophy in all its parts.[17]

And to what extent were innovations publicised in treatises taken up and used in practice? Jones's much advertised English system probably found little sustained use in the world of commerce. But what about Degrange's combined journal-ledger, first described in 1804,[18] and imitated, modified or unmodified, in many publications in the first half of the nineteenth century, when it came to be known, quite arbitrarily, as the 'American' system? Or what about the combined wastebook-journal (or so-called 'marginal journal') described by Malcolm in 1731?[19] A further question is whether any inferences can be drawn from the fact that there were best-selling treatises in English and French published in the eighteenth century (e.g. Mair and de la Porte),[20] but not in German or Italian. And, to go back a century or so before that time, does the fact that two of the best Italian books on the double-entry system, those by Pietra and Flori, described the system applied to the affairs of monasteries mean that monasteries or monastic orders in Italy in fact used the system widely?[21] And if they did, what is the explanation?

I could go on cataloguing deficiencies in our knowledge of accounting in the period I have taken as my example, depressing as this may be—

---

[13]W. T. Baxter, 'Accounting in Colonial America', in A. C. Littleton and B. S. Yamey (eds.), *Studies in the History of Accounting*, London, 1956, p. 279. According to Harrington, 'most wholesale houses [in New York] *apparently* used double-entry bookkeeping' (italics added), a guarded statement: V. D. Harrington, *The New York Merchant on the Eve of the Revolution*, New York, 1935, p. 96. For France, Meyer's study of eighteenth-century ship-owners of Nantes includes a useful attempt to assess the accounting practices in Brittany at the time: J. Meyer, *L'Armement Nantais dans la deuxième Moitié du XVIIIe Siècle*, Paris, 1969, pp. 119 *et s\. q.*

[14]For example, the Company of General [Tax] Farmers in eighteenth-century France at one time adopted double entry, and abandonded it quite soon: G. T. Matthews, *The Royal General Farms in Eighteenth Century France*, New York, 1958, pp. 73 and 218.

[15]According to Wagner, who wrote early in the nineteenth century, most of the teachers of bookkeeping in Germany were mercenaries, including bankrupts and unsuccessful business men, who did not care whether their pupils learnt anything so long as they received their fees. Wagner also was emphatic that boys should not be taught bookkeeping until they became apprenticed to merchants. Otherwise, such tuition was damaging or at best purposeless and useless: A. Wagner, *Neues vollständiges und allgemeines Lehrbuch des Buchhaltens*, Magdeburg, 1802, pp. 15 and 17. Goodacre, who wrote at about the same time as Wagner, was more cautious: 'But though a short course of Book-keeping at School may be useful, it is the opinion of many commercial men, that but little of a Schoolboy's time ought to be employed in the subject. The author confesses that he has long been of this opinion...'. R. Goodacre, *A Treatise on Book-keeping*, London, 1811, p. 4. Mr Michael Bywater kindly drew my attention to this unusual book.

[16]Degrange on pre-Degrangian methods of teaching: '... on employait le plus souvent, sans aucun fruit, des années entières à ce qu'on appelait alors l'étude des parties doubles, par la raison que ces moyens d'une routine aveugle et machinale, loin d'être utiles à l'enseignement, ne peuvent que lui êntre nuisibles, et qu'en confondant et compliquant toutes les idées, ils suffisent pour créer des difficultés qui paraissent insurmontables'; E. Degrange, *La Tenue des Livres Rendue Facile*, 11th ed., Paris, 1819, p. vi.

[17]R. Gascon in P. Chaunu and R. Gascon, *Histoire Économique et Sociale de la France*, book 1, vol. 1, Paris, 1977, p. 315.

[18]E. Degrange, *Supplement a la Tenue des Livres Rendue Facile*, Paris, 1804.

[19]A. Malcolm, *A Treatise of Book-keeping*, London, 1731, pp. 30–31. Malcolm refers to the combined wastebook-journal as 'a new Method, which I have found practised by some eminent Traders' (p. 28). J. Mair says of this method that 'There are some Moderns who have got into another Fashion'. J. Mair, *Book-keeping Methodiz'd*, Edinburgh, 1736, p. 11.

[20]J. Mair, *op. cit.*; M. De la Porte, *La Science des Negocians et Teneurs de Livres*, Paris, 1704. Each of these books was re-issued many times during the eighteenth century.

[21]A. Pietra, *Indrizzo degli Economi*, Mantua, 1586; L. Flori, *Trattato del Modo di Tenere il Libro Doppio Domestico*, Palermo, 1636.

and misleading as it is, in that I am not saying much about what I think we *do* know. But before concluding this part of my paper, let me quickly note a few more questions.

Who were the bookkeepers or account-keepers (to use Peele's term) in our selected period? Many merchants kept their own accounts. Others, especially in Holland, it appears, had their wives act as bookkeepers—a salutary form of division of labour which the Englishman Sir Josiah Child envied for his own country.[22] But there were also bookkeepers or account-keepers who worked for others. What were their origins and backgrounds? Were there differences between the accounts kept by salaried bookkeepers and those kept by the business men themselves? Was the spread of the double-entry system associated with the employment of specialist bookkeepers, trained in the mysteries of the subject and eager to demonstrate their skill? Was the double entry system sometimes or often foisted on businesses which would have done better with something much simpler?[23] It would possibly be revealing if one could now examine instances of changes in accounting systems and procedures in the same enterprise, and could link these changes with other changes such as the growth of the business, the taking on of salaried bookkeepers, and so on. In all, a history of accounting in the period (or in any period) without some knowledge of the actors—those for whom as well as those by whom the records were kept—must be rather anaemic and thin. I would certainly like to learn more about the (at present) somewhat shadowy figures who, in the words of one of them, 'justly made up' or settled 'all kinds of intricate and confus'd accounts'.[24] What did these apparently free-lance individuals do? And how often were they called in to act as accounting physicians? Probably quite often. Abraham de Graaf has a chapter in his treatise

entitled 'How to salvage confused books, at least as far as possible'.[25] According to Jürgen Kocka, writing of early industrialisation in Germany, bookkeepers who were taken into employment some years after the establishment of manufacturing enterprises by artisans often found great chaos in the accounts (although it may be unwise to infer that their owners were necessarily also in the dark).[26] The story of contentious accounts and fraudulent accounts should indeed be an important, and at times entertaining, component of a general history of accounting through the ages, and especially of the activities and functions of auditors—from Chaucer's reeve to the McKesson and Robbins case, and beyond.[27]

Again, to what extent did the practice of accounting in the period depend upon forces operating from outside (i.e. coming from outside the enterprises and their particular requirements)? For example, in Italy in the earliest part of our period was the use of double entry widespread because 'the habit of precise calculation was ingrained in Italian life'? Was the record-keeping by Italian merchants and heads of households partly a reflection of 'the self-consciousness of Renaissance man' (to quote Peter Burke)?[28] We may never know with any degree of certainty. But a general historian of accounting should concern himself with such questions, and discover and make use of relevant evidence; or use his creative imagination, which is part of the historian's equipment. And one should also have to try to answer the question whether externally generated ideas and notions and enquiries might not have been rubbed off on to accounting in practice. It has been posited that the French Physiocrats, in their enquiries elaborating and then verifying their *Tableau économique*, may have been 'respon-

---

[22]Sir Josiah Child, *A New Discourse of Trade*, London, 1693.

[23]Fulton referred to the reverse possibility, namely that businessmen, believing that the double entry system was designed for wholesale merchants, 'on entering into life as tradesmen, shop-keepers, or manufacturers, ... are fain to take up with any plan of account, however imperfect, adopted by any person in a similar line of business...; and unnecessary labour, uncertainty, error and often endless litigation, are the consequences'. Fulton attributes the widespread belief that double entry is for wholesale merchants to the 'mode of instruction, by what is termed *familiar example*' in treatises which generally 'exemplify the transactions of a wholesale-merchant': J. W. Fulton, *British-Indian Book-keeping*, London, 1800, pp. xiv–xv.

[24]H. Stephens, *Italian Book-keeping, Reduced into an Art*, London, 1735, Advertisement.

[25]A. de Graaf, *Instructie van het Italiaans Boekhouden*, Hardewyk, 1693, pp. 98–9.

[26]J. Kocka, *Unternehmer in der deutschen Industrialisierung*, Göttingen, 1975, p. 74. It may be unwise to conclude from an apparent confusion in the accounts that the owner of the business himself was confused and ill-informed about his affairs. Everaert has shown how the writing-up of account-books of Flemish merchants trading in Cadiz was often in arrears for many months. Nevertheless, the details recorded in the various auxiliary account-books, which were kept regularly, enabled the merchant to control his affairs effectively: J. Everaert, *De Internationale en Koloniale Handel der Vlaamse Firma's te Cadiz*, Bruges, 1973, pp. 68–71.

[27]The following is a sample selection of books which describe, *inter alia*, conflicts involving accounts: W. Brulez, *De Firma della Faille en de Internationale Handel van Vlaamse Firma's in de 16e Eeuw*, Brussels, 1959; E. N. Hartley, *Ironworks on the Saugus*, Norman, 1957; D. Miquelon, *Dugard of Rouen*, Montreal, 1978.

[28]P. Burke, *Tradition and Innovation in Renaissance Italy*, London, 1974, p. 235.

sible for decisive advances in the way farmers kept their accounts'.[29] (Incidentally, for a later period than I have concentrated on, Murray Wells has most effectively traced the various sources of influence which gave rise to the development of the allocation of common costs in industrial accounting in the second half of the nineteenth century.)[30]

How accounting information was used

The uses and significance of accounting through the ages will be that part of any general history of accounting which will appeal to the widest range of readers. For, as is well known, considerable *general* significance has been attributed to accounting and accounting systems; and references to bookkeeping and accounting (often wrong in mundane but tell-tale details[31]) can be found in works of economic history, of social history, and, indeed, of the history of ideas and culture.

But first things first. How did the owners of businesses use their accounts? For unless we understand this, the wider significance of accounting will be impossible to determine. Quite obviously, at all times businessmen have used their account-books to give them detailed pieces of information necessary for the efficient administration and control of assets, such as debts, cash, and goods, and for purposes of rendering accounts, in situations and contexts where accountability was involved. Sometimes, of course, their records have been so ill-kept or inaccurate as to mislead themselves, and possibly others as well.

The diversity of the accounting methods and devices used in connection with the necessary but humdrum recording of the details of business op-erations is itself fascinating.[32] But far greater interest attaches to the use of the more synoptic and abstract products of accounting processes and transformations.

Here we are on more difficult ground. Sometimes fairly specific evidence has survived of the particular use to which such material was put, in connection with the making of particular business decisions. Robert Loder's farm account-book of the early seventeenth century is a case in point.[33] Sometimes, also, the material itself may reveal something about the uses to which it was put—or rather not put. The early balance accounts of the Medici Bank are little booklets listing ledger account balances. They are not trim summaries of items, purposively arranged and grouped, to reveal facets or implications otherwise obscured by the details of a myriad of individual account balances. Ten Have rightly warned accounting historians not to be misled by summaries of original documents prepared much later by economic historians for their own purposes.[34] Skipping the centuries, we have been told that the earliest surviving balance sheet, for 1834, of the Dowlais Iron Company extends over 14 pages, and has but one sub-heading.[35] At the other extreme, there are balance accounts of the seventeenth and eighteenth centuries with only two laconic entries: 'To Sundries' and 'By Sundries'.

But often the document or calculation does not speak for itself. Then the historian has to try to probe into the surrounding circumstances for clues. I am sure that there are many collections of records, especially for the last 250 years. which deserve careful study from this point of view by the accounting historian. And good business histories are another underused resource. Thus Neil McKendrick has been able to establish quite precisely the use to which the manufacturing potter, Josiah Wedgwood, put his *ad hoc* cost analyses of

[29]J-C. Perrot, 'La Comptabilité des Entreprises Agricoles dans l'Économie Physiocratique', *Annales: Economies Sociétés Civilisations*, vol. 33, 1978; quotation in text from English summary, p. 678.
[30]M. C. Wells, *Accounting for Common Costs*, Urbana, 1978.
[31]Thus Nussbaum writes, incorrectly, that the French Code of Commerce of 1673 established double-entry bookkeeping as a general obligation of the more important businessmen, and that the Code enjoined all merchants and men of affairs to keep a book to show, among other things, 'the money invested in their establishments': F. L. Nussbaum, *The Triumph of Science and Reason 1660–1685*, New York, 1962, pp. 202–3. The following statement appears in the English version of Max Weber's famous book on economic history: 'The device of the balance was first insisted upon by the Dutch theorist Simon Stevin in the year 1698': M. Weber, *General Economic History* (translated by F. H. Knight), paperback edition, New York, 1961, p. 207.

[32]Cf. Goodacre, *op. cit.*, p. 5: 'The art of Book-keeping was no doubt originally invented, in some respects, to ease the memory, and, in others, to preserve by visible marks those transactions which otherwise could not be retained ... The illiterate Milkwoman frequently knows as well the state of her affairs, by the chalks on her Dairy-door, as the Merchant does his by his ponderous volumes'.
[33]G. E. Fussell (ed.), *Robert Loder's Farm Accounts, 1610–1620*, Camden Third Series, vol. 53, London, 1936.
[34]O. ten Have, *The History of Accountancy*, translated by A. van Seventer, Palo Alto, 1976, p. 44, n. 11.
[35]J. R. Edwards and C. Baber, 'Dowlais Iron Company: Accounting Policies and Procedures for Profit Measurement and Reporting Purposes', *Accounting and Business Research*, Spring, 1979, p. 141.

the early 1770s.[36] Failing such supports, the accounting historian must use his imagination—with the risks of unhistorical projecting of the past into the different present, and of turning hypotheses into evidence. It is altogether too tempting, in the absence of other information, to infer the use of an accounting record from the apparent class or type of the document itself—a temptation which is all the stronger if one accepts the common view that accounting practices are 'but the outcome of continued efforts to meet the necessities of trade as they gradually developed'[37]—a view which, as usually expressed, is wholly inadequate in its failure to specify the particular necessity and the accounting change, and a view which leaves no room either for the autonomous development of new practices or for the obstinate survival of obsolete practices and procedures (a theme illustrated in miniature, as it were, by Hatfield).[38]

The interesting questions of the use of accounting material for decision-making relate primarily to situations in which the decision-maker is some distance removed from the scene of detailed business activities, so that he is obliged to rely, for his view of these activities, upon what he is told about them. It is then, and probably only then, that the more summary, abstract or synthetic accounting documents come into their own. I need not dwell on their positive importance in this context. But pathological cases are more revealing than normal cases. It is of great interest for the historian to know whether and how often and in what particular circumstances the wrong business decisions have been made because accounts and accounting statements served as a distorting or concealing veil interposed between reality and the decision-maker, or because an entry in a ledger account or an item in an accounting statement necessarily conveys to the 'distant' reader rather less information than was known by the person who initiated the action behind that entry or item. Evidently one needs to know what other sources of information were available to the decision-taker; whether he was aware of the conventions or practices underlying the accounting material available to him; and

also how important for the decision other (non-accounting) circumstances and influences happened to have been.

I do not think we have got very far into this range of issues, although the work of Thomas Johnson, for example, is valuable and illuminating.[39] Thomas J. Kreps gave the example in the 1920s of an efficient divisional manager in a chemical company who was almost dismissed by the owners (a bank) because his division always showed a loss—the result of an arbitrary allocation of completely fixed common costs. He kept his job when someone, who knew his worth, changed the basis of allocation, to something equally arbitrary.[40] We need to know how common or uncommon such or similar cases of unintentional misinformation have been before we can answer important questions, and assess, for example, the significance, since the rise of large-scale enterprise, of financial accounting and cost accounting in matters such as the quality of entrepreneurial decisions, the determination of the volume and allocation of investible funds, and the course of business cycles—to take three evidently important subjects of wide economic interest. In the same context, we also need to know how the choice among different accounting policies has been made, and the policies implemented, in corporate enterprises over the last hundred years or so.

How does one reconstruct the circumstances surrounding past entrepreneurial decisions, the influences bearing upon the decision-makers, and the ways their minds worked? I do not want to minimise the difficulties. Yet we should nevertheless have to attempt such acts of reconstruction—or else our history will be side-stepping interesting and important issues, perhaps the *most* important. I am aware one can easily misread the signs—as I confess I did when I looked at a painting of 1806 by Sir Thomas Lawrence which seemed to represent a scene of decision-making in the presence of accounting information: perhaps the perfect illustration for the core of Sombart's thesis. The painting shows Sir Francis Baring (of the banking house), his brother and his son-in-law

---

[36] N. McKendrick, 'Josiah Wedgwood and Cost Accounting in the Industrial Revolution', *Economic History Review*, vol. 23, reprinted in B. S. Yamey (ed.) *The Historical Development of Accounting*, New York, 1978.

[37] R. H. Montgomery, foreword to E. Peragallo, *Origin and Development of Double Entry Bookkeeping*, New York, 1938.

[38] H. R. Hatfield, 'Accounting Trivia', *Accounting Review*, vol. 15, 1940.

[39] H. T. Johnson, 'Management Accountancy in an Early Integrated Industry: E. I. du Pont de Nemours Powder Company, 1903–1912', *Business History Review*, Summer 1975; 'Management Accounting in an Early Multidivision Organization: General Motors in the 1920s', *Business History Review*, Winter, 1978.

[40] T. J. Kreps, 'Joint Costs in the Chemical Industry', *Quarterly Journal of Economics*, vol. 44, 1930, quoted in R. S. Edwards, 'The Rationale of Cost Accounting', in D. Solomons (ed.) *Studies in Costing*, London, 1952, p. 99.

at a desk on which there is a large open ledger. Sir Francis has an intent look on his face while the others are attentive. His left hand is raised in an apparently significant gesture. But I have since learned that the position of the hand reflects no more than the fact that Sir Francis was deaf. (The ledger is open at the account of 'Hope & Co', the famous Amsterdam banking firm.)[41]

Accounting in a wider setting

Let me now, in conclusion, proceed further in search of the wider historical significance of accounting, way beyond the significance of the accounts for the individual enterprise. Here I need do no more than recall Werner Sombart's thesis which links double entry bookkeeping with economic rationality and capitalism. On this occasion I will restrain myself and not repeat what I have said before on this subject, nor add to it. But perhaps not quite..... In a recent interesting and provocative book, Alan Macfarlane, an economic and social historian, sees *any* carefully kept set of accounts—whether by double entry or not—as evidence of 'a sophisticated and "rational" approach', with economic and social implications and consequences similar to those attributed by Sombart to double entry. Macfarlane, indeed, sees in the estate accounting of the manorial system in England the 'rationality, sophisticated accounting, emphasis on profit, and universal translatability of every item into an exact cash equivalent which would have surprised Weber'[42]—and presumably Sombart also. (Incidentally, the Italian word *ragione*, a word of several meanings, can mean both 'reason' and also 'account'.[43] And again, incidentally, Oschinsky has contended that the system of manorial accounting used in medieval England enabled landowners, whenever it was more profitable to do so, to farm their own lands directly rather than through tenants, whilst in Germany this was not possible because nothing like the system was used there).[44] Conversely, however, the distinguished historian of classical antiquity, Moses Finley, has included accounting records and calculations among his evidence to establish the conclusion that 'investment in land... was never in antiquity a matter of systematic, calculated policy, of what Weber called economic rationality'.[45]

Perhaps the notion of economic rationality has by now become disablingly fuzzy. Nevertheless, here are deep and difficult waters for the accounting historian and—dare I say it yet again?—much more work remains to be done. But we may as well go deeper still. And let us note how some historians, not accounting historians, have looked upon the double entry technique.

Samuel Edgerton Jr., is an art historian. In a recent book he notes that by the fifteenth century 'merchants and bankers of Florence... were keeping the best-ordered books in Europe, and controlled far-flung business empires through an intricate system of debit and credit accounting'. He then asks—and implies a positive answer: 'Did not these tight-fisted, practical-minded businessmen find themselves more and more disposed to a visual world that would accord with the tidy principles of mathematical order that they applied to their bank ledgers?'[46] Did their modes of thought and mental habits, that is to say, not make it easier for linear perspective to be introduced into early Renaissance painting and for such paintings to be acceptable? More generally, did not the interests and mental habits of merchants and bookkeepers help to promote the naturalism evident in the art of Renaissance Italy?[47]

One can quite easily think up similar juxtapositionings—as, for example, this one put forward, but not seriously, by the medievalist, Robert Lopez: 'One might compare the clarity and symmetry of Renaissance double-entry books of accounting to the clarity and symmetry of

---

[41] M. Levey, *Sir Thomas Lawrence: 1769–1830*, London, 1979, catalogue entry no. 23. A mezzotint by J. Ward of the painting is reproduced in M. G. Buist, *At Spes non Fracta: Hope & Co., 1770–1815*, The Hague, 1974, p. 464.

[42] A. Macfarlane, *The Origins of English Individualism*, Oxford, 1978, p. 152, n. 93. Aersten in his recent stimulating article on Weber's *Wirtschaftsethos* also links bookkeeping and rationality, but gives pride of place to double-entry bookkeeping: J. A. Aersten, 'Burger en Beroep in de Middeleeuwen', *Economisch en Sociaal-Historisch Jaarboek*, vol. 41, 1978.

[43] See P. Burke, *op. cit.*, pp. 234–5.

[44] D. Oschinsky, *Walter of Henley and other Treatises on Estate Management and Accounting*, Oxford, 1971, p. 213.

[45] M. I. Finley, *The Ancient Economy*, London, 1973, p. 117. Confidence in Finley's conclusion is weakened, however, by the fact that he instances in its support 'the complete absence of the concept of amortization' and the 'amalgamation' of personal possessions and business property in statements of capital. The same would be true, however, of, say, business accounts in seventeenth century Britain.

[46] S. Y. Edgerton, Jr., *The Renaissance Rediscovery of Linear Perspective*, paperback edition, New York, 1976, p. 39.

[47] Leonardo Olschki denies the connection. He adduces evidence which satisfies him 'that the artistic naturalism of those generations did not derive from the interests and mental habits of merchants and bookkeepers, as is sometimes represented, but was rather the expression of a general spiritual desire for order, balance, clarity and truth': L. Olschki, *The Genius of Italy*, London, 1950, p. 295.

Renaissance buildings'. And one can as easily ridicule this type of playing around with manifestations of the supposed *Zeitgeist*—as Lopez did when he quoted from an examination answer he once had to grade: 'Double-entry bookkeeping in the Medici Bank goaded Michelangelo to conceive and accomplish the Medici Chapel; contemplation of the Medici Chapel in turn spurred the bankers to a more muscular management of credit'.[48] We must not let our imaginations run riot even when we are obliged to use them: a clear appreciation of the *available* facts of accounting practices is often enough to prevent such rampaging.

Again, as touched on earlier, might not attitudes towards (say) double entry bookkeeping in some cases partly have reflected general cultural attitudes? Michael Baxandall, a perceptive art historian, has suggested that successful merchants in Augsburg at the beginning of the sixteenth century might have been more receptive to the 'Italian art of double-entry accounting' because they were receptive to Italianate ideas and Italianate persons of various sorts. He refers in support to a passage in Matthäus Schwarz's celebrated manuscript of the early sixteenth century which, he claims, eulogises double entry bookkeeping 'in a tone close to Dürer's account of modern scientific painting'.[49] Such parallels are often stimulating, but often fragile. Here one can note briefly that Schwarz's manuscript deals both with 'Italian' and also with 'German' bookkeeping, and his encomium on the art is couched in general terms

to cover bookkeeping generally.[50] Moreover, Augsburg's foremost merchant family, the Fugger, for whom Schwarz worked as '*Buchhalter*', appear not to have used the Italian system of bookkeeping—although they certainly commissioned several Italianate works of art.

But to return to accounting and business. May it not be possible that the widespread adoption and acceptance of the double entry system of business recording has served to impose some sort of constraint on the way in which accountants and businessmen have come to view the business world or aspects of business operations? And that this blinkering or disciplining (according to taste) has had its effects on business decisions? I am sceptical. In a rather different field, that of the influence of language on thought and ideas (where the influence might be thought to be both potent and pervasive), recent scholarship seems to show that 'we are, in our general metaphysics, far less slaves of our syntax than the language-enthusiasts have claimed. It seems that our visions can defy the bias of our grammar'.[51]

All this, nevertheless, opens up an intriguing realm for speculation, possibly even for heady speculation by otherwise sober-sided historians of accounting, as sober-sided as the modern professional accountant. Such speculation would, however, be a far cry from their more usual concerns, such as their concerns with, say, the valuation of merchandise inventories in mercantile accounting in eighteenth-century Europe, or with the impact on business decisions of Securities and Exchange Commission accounting regulations or of the Financial Accounting Standards Board, as regards, for instance, the treatment of gains or losses on foreign exchange.[52] However, if I may repeat a point made earlier in this paper, discussion of the wider economic as well as non-economic significance of accounting in a particular period will be much more fruitful if it can proceed on the basis of well-established facts about the details of accounting practices in that period.

---

[48]R. S. Lopez, 'Hard times and Investment in Culture', in *The Renaissance: Six Essays*, paperback edition, New York, 1962, pp. 44 and 29. The art historian Arnold Hauser has claimed common significance for a series of supposed manifestations of the Renaissance spirit: 'The principles of unity which now [in the Renaissance] become authoritative in art, the unification of space and the unified standards of proportions, the restriction of the artistic representation to one single theme and the concentration of the composition into one immediately intelligible form, are also in accordance with this new rationalism. They express the same dislike for the incalculable and the uncontrollable as the economy of the same period with its emphasis on planning, expediency and calculability; they are creations of the same spirit which makes its way in the organisation of labour, in trading methods, the credit system and double-entry book-keeping, in methods of government, in diplomacy and warfare': A. Hauser, *The Social History of Art*, paperback edition, London, 1962, vol. 2, pp. 11–12.

[49]M. Baxandall, *The Limewood Sculptors of Renaissance Germany*, London, 1980, p. 136.

[50]The passage in Schwarz's manuscript quoted by Baxandall could apply equally to the two 'bookkeepings' described by Schwarz.

[51]Review by E. Gellner, *Times Literary Supplement*, 15 August, 1980, p. 911.

[52]On this particular topic, see for example J. M. Burns, *Accounting Standards and International Finance*, Washington D.C., 1976.

ACCOUNTING IN THE MIDDLE AGES,
500 TO 1500

ACCOUNTING IN THE MIDDLE AGES, 500-1500

Accounts and accounting statements take a variety of forms, vary greatly in scope and content, and may serve a variety of purposes. They range from records of detailed information useful for the control and administration of assets such as money or debts, to statements that summarise and classify receipts and expenditures, profits and losses, or assets and liabilities – synoptic statements conceivably helpful in the formulation of major financial or economic decisions.

Surviving medieval accounts display considerable variety as regards account keeper (cleric or layman), content, order or lack of it, regularity, numeral system (Roman or Arabic), language (Latin or vernacular), form (roll, book, or loose records), and material (parchment, paper, or wax tablet). They were generated in a variety of contexts and within a diversity of institutions. Nevertheless, excluding those of commercial enterprises, most of the remaining accounting materials exhibit one common feature: they were created as part of a process in which a subordinate agent or steward "accounted" to his superior or principal – that is, a process in which the subordinate from time to time sought to justify his activities on behalf of his superior, and to determine the remaining debt owed to or owed by the superior.

Stewardship accounting was likely to exist wherever the delegated activities were extensive or complex, the superior or principal often was absent, and literate clerks were available to compose the accounts. The purpose of such accounting was the same as that ascribed by de Ste. Croix to Greek and Roman accounting: "The whole purpose of ancient accounting was...to keep accurate records of acquisitions and outgoings, in money and kind, and to expose any losses due to dishonesty and negligence" (de Ste. Croix, 1956, p. 38).

Accounts alone would not be satisfactory for this purpose. Entries in the accounts would have to be examined to determine what lay behind them, and to establish that all revenues due to the principal had been collected or otherwise satisfactorily accounted for, and that all expenditures by the agent had been properly incurred or authorised. This examination of the stewardship accounts was the audit. As the word indicates, the examination of the "accountant" (agent) by the auditor(s) was oral: this was so partly because accountants or auditors might be illiterate, and also because "reading was still primarily oral rather than visual" (Clanchy, 1979, p. 215).

Basically a stewardship account was an account of the reporting steward's receipts and expenditures of money or goods on behalf of his principal. But it was not invariably quite so simple. An account might record among "receipts" the full amount of an item that should have been received even though it had not been received in full. Or an entry on the "receipts" side might record the unspent part of an authorised item of expenditure entered in full on the "payments" side. Thus the terms "charge" and "discharge" are more accurate than "receipts" and "payments". The balance

on an account represented the amount due to or from the steward,

and it was in no sense the profit or loss on his activities.

Stewardship accounting was prescribed in the Carolingian

Capitulare de villis, ca. 800, issued partly in an attempt to

eliminate improprieties in the administration by the stewards

(*iudices*) of the royal estates and partly to encourage production.

Several paragraphs in the capitulary concern quantitative returns

to be submitted to the palace - for instance, "Let the stewards

give us an accounting of the male and female goats and of their

horns and skins..." Since many of the stewards were illiterate,

Wolfgang Metz believes that accounts were not rendered to the

palace, but given verbally to the travelling *missi*. The *missi* or

their clerks would draw up the accounts from the information

supplied (Metz, 1960, p. 82). Later instructions required

additional returns from the stewards - for example, of the wool and

flax issued to women on the royal domain and of the number of

garments produced. It is not known how scrupulously these various

instructions were carried out.

The papal accounting system serves to illustrate several

points. Outside the patrimonies and the states of the Church,

revenues were collected by officials appointed by the pope. They

had wide powers. "The responsibility of the collectors was enforced

mainly by the accounts which they were compelled to render to the

camera" (Lunt, 1934, vol. 1, p. 47). They had to submit their accounts in person in Rome (or Avignon), at first whenever summoned and later commonly regularly every two years. They had to produce vouchers and other evidence to support their accounting. Members of the college of clerks responsible to the *camerarius*, or chamberlain, audited the accounts in detail and prepared them for final approval by the *camerarius* or the cameral council.

The collector had some incentive to keep accurate records because his personal assets were at risk as security, a feature of personal responsibility also found in other administrative systems, such as municipal government and the English manorial system. There were ample opportunities for fraud in the collectorates, and the *camera* was aware of them. A papal bull of 1404 recounted possible types of fraud, including reporting as arrears to be collected sums that had already been collected, and making vacant benefices available to accomplices at low prices. Multiplicity of currencies also facilitated the duping of cameral officials. Moreover, the requirement of regular accounting at the *camera* was widely disregarded, and the *camera* found it necessary from time to time to send envoys to conduct audits and investigations on site. There were several collectors, like Jean de Palmis in southern France, who began as poor men and soon became wealthy. One is reminded of Chaucer's reeve of the manor who, although also subject to account and audit, "koude better than his lord purchace./ Ful riche he was astored pryvely".

The cameral treasurer, responsible for the receipt and payment of moneys, had to account annually to the *camerarius* on the

basis of his account-book, the *introitus et exitus*, the entries
in which were based on a chronologically-entered journal. The
depository, usually a firm of bankers appointed by the pope,
stored and handled the cash, and had to render accounts regularly
to the *camera*. The *camerarius*, the highest financial officer and
a person close to the pope, in turn had to render an account when
he gave up the office; and if this was satisfactory, he was
released by the pope from further financial responsibility.

"In medieval administrative systems finance and judicature
went hand in hand" (Lunt, 1934, vol. 1, p. 21). This was true of
the papal camera. It was also true, for example, of the royal
exchequer in England and of corresponding institutions in Western
Europe, such as the *Chambre des comptes* in France.

Much is known about accounting in the exchequer of the
English kings because copious records have survived and there is
available the manuscript *Dialogus de scaccario*, written toward the
end of the twelfth century by Richard Fitzneale, treasurer of
England and bishop of London. Some features of early exchequer
accounting may have been superimposed upon a pre-Conquest illiterate
method of account-keeping by means of notches on sticks (Johnson,
1950, p. xxxv). Other features of the functioning of the exchequer
may have been influenced by the constitution and operations of the
duana of King Roger of Sicily, which in turn may have been derived
from the practices of the Fatimid *dīwān*. (But such connections
are highly speculative; and English practice may have influenced
the Sicilian in some respects.)

The English medieval exchequer developed out of the *curia regis*, and was entrusted with financial and judicial responsibilities. The accounting and audit arrangements are of interest here. The sheriffs and other royal officers annually rendered their accounts before the barons of the exchequer and their specialist staff. Proceedings took place around a large table covered with a cloth marked into squares. This was the "chessboard" or abacus on which an officer, the calculator, placed counters, the number and location of which indicated sums of money. Additions and subtractions were performed on the exchequer board in a manner visible and comprehensible to all present, the object being to establish, in effect, the accountant's balance vis-à-vis the crown. The accountant produced supporting vouchers and tallies, and his explanations could be challenged and adjudicated. The resulting accounts were enrolled to form the pipe rolls, many of which have survived, the earliest being that of 1130.

The contents of the exchequer rolls underwent modifications from time to time. Thus, when the number of debtors to the crown had increased greatly, space was saved and greater clarity achieved in the pipe rolls by consolidating many otherwise separate receipts as single entries, and by removing details of certain categories of revenue to separate rolls.

Just as the sheriffs had to account to the exchequer, so the treasurer and chamberlains of the exchequer from time to time had to account to special commissioners appointed by the king. At first these commissioners were men of high rank in the court, but by the

fourteenth century this type of audit was being performed by an
official of the treasury.

The main accounting and auditing features of the early
exchequer system were found also in Flemish, Capetian and Norman
financial institutions. It appears that by the eleventh century,
written accounts and elaborate financial administration, previously
unnecessary, had to be introduced. Common problems and links
between the countries ensured that basically similar solutions
came to be adopted, although there were minor differences in early
practice. For instance, in France accounts were rendered three
times a year; in England, Normandy, and Flanders the final account
only once yearly (though there was usually also a preliminary account).
Payments into the treasury were made more frequently.

The Teutonic Knights had elaborate accounting and auditing
arrangements, two features of which are of interest. First, from
the middle of the fourteenth century the officers of the various
establishments of the order had to compile inventories of the assets
and liabilities to be handed over to their successors. Copies were
sent to the headquarters in Marienburg (now Malbork, Poland), where
the information was entered in a book. Second, the *Treszler* in
Marienburg kept detailed records of the money transactions he
handled. Annual accounts were prepared from preliminary records,
which were probably made on wax tablets and destroyed when no longer
required. These annual accounts, partly organised according to the
type of transaction and partly chronological, were submitted to the
Groszkomtur (grand-commander) for approval.

Many accounts of the finances of town and city administrations survive from the thirteenth century on. The elected or appointed treasurers and other accounting officials submitted their accounts periodically to the magistrates, to other scrutineers, or in some cases to assemblies of citizens. Like the similar accounts of other governmental institutions, these accounts, written on rolls or in books, tended to improve in terms of systemisation and order in the course of the later Middle Ages. (It may be noted, in passing, that Leonardo Fibonacci, author of an influential work on arithmetic, *Liber abaci (1202)*, probably at one time was examiner of the Pisan municipal accounts. The account-books of the *biccherna*, the Sienese treasury, are unique among municipal account-books in having wooden covers adorned with paintings by local artists.)

For effective audit the examiners of papal, royal or municipal accounts required independent information about the receipts due from the accountants. For this purpose, as well as for other administrative reasons, lists of amounts due from tenants, revenue farmers, and taxpayers were prepared. For example, following a practice initiated in ancient Egypt, land registers were compiled for revenue administration in the Byzantine Empire. Several Carolingian surveys or inventories of manors have survived – the polyptych of estates near Paris belonging to the abbey of St.-Germain-des-Prés, compiled early in the ninth century, is an elaborate example. A copy of the Domesday Book of 1086 (itself developed in an Anglo-Saxon administrative context) was kept in

the English exchequer, although the extent of its use is debatable.
In Sicily a similar record was compiled in 1140.

The auditors in the English exchequer also used information
contained in earlier pipe rolls as a basis for checking entries
in the current accounts under audit. They also had the up-to-date
rotulus exactorius showing farms due from the sheriffs. In the
Normandy of the Angevin dukes, the *extractus memorandorum* listed
under each district certain debts and revenues from land to be
collected by the officer in charge. In 1192 the papal *camerarius*
Cencio compiled the first *liber censuum*, which listed by provinces
and dioceses those who owed census and the amounts due.

How well informed about the state of their finances were
the central headquarters of such far-flung organisations as the
papacy and the royal states? Evidently the numerous accounts
rendered by local agents and others provided a mass of detailed
information. But the content and form of these accounts reflected
their limited purpose, and not all revenues or expenditures
necessarily flowed into or out of the various treasuries. The
French exchequer rolls of the twelfth century and the summary
accounts of 1202 "are very confused....It would be difficult from
these rolls to find the total revenue collected by one man or the
total revenue given by one source" (Strayer, 1932, p. 36). During
the reign of Louis IX, the centralisation of authority in the hands
of the *baillis* and the gradual development of classification of
revenues and expenditures in the accounts represented substantial
improvements.

The *camera* of the Avignonese popes had no "clear and immediate knowledge of the overall state of the papal finances", but "it had a detailed, if delayed knowledge of its revenues, and had absolute control over their use" (Favier, 1966, p. 92).

This centralisation of papal finance and accounting did not last, "since in the fifteenth century the centralised system of book-keeping" of Avignon broke down (Partner, 1960, p. 256). But summaries of the accounts, comprehensive in scope, could be compiled when required. The so-called budget of the Roman Church of 1480-1481 is an example. A surviving fragment of an account reveals that in 1221, towards the end of the reign of Philip II, a general recapitulation of the French royal receipts and payments was drawn up. Unlike that of the earlier surviving French account of 1202, it was not the purpose of the account of 1221 to control the payments made by *baillis* and other accountants; rather, it was to provide a review of the royal finances, and may well be the earliest surviving so-called budget of northern Europe. (It was not a budget in the modern sense.) The emperors of the Holy Roman Empire, by contrast, generally seem to have displayed "remarkable ignorance of the imperial domains and the royal revenues" (Schubert, 1979, p. 147).

The preceding discussion should dispel any erroneous impression that accounting information was recorded and compiled solely for the purpose of rendering accounts of stewardship. Two more commonplace examples may be useful here. The murage and pavage accounts of Shrewsbury, England, have survived from as

early as 1256. It is evident that each account is "a public
record, not a private justification; it is, so to speak, itself
part of the works for which the murage pays" (Martin, 1963, p. 135).
And the administration of the Duke of Brabant in 1358 kept a
ledger of current accounts.

A much-studied class of stewardship accounts are the
manorial accounts of ecclesiastic and lay owners of large estates
in England. Many have survived, and are valuable sources for
economic historians. The accounts of the thirteenth and fourteenth
centuries are especially useful because demesne farming (the
direct conduct by the owner of agricultural activities through
local agents) was widespread in England, unlike the rest of Europe.
Agricultural estate accounting of continental Europe has not
attracted systematic study, and does not appear to have followed
any particular pattern.

In England the local agent was the reeve or bailiff
responsible for a manor. He was in charge of the manorial demesne
and also collected rents from tenants. He rendered an annual
written account, examined locally by itinerant auditors responsible
to the owner. The system of written accounts probably developed
out of an earlier system of oral accounting.

In the period from (roughly) 1270 to 1350, manorial
accounts were fairly standardised, the result of exchanges of ideas
and methods among owners and officers, the circulation of specimen
accounts and manuscript treatises, and possibly also the regular

courses for clerks taught at Oxford and elsewhere, which almost
certainly included instruction in the compilation of manorial
accounts. The typical account roll is described below (Harvey,
1976, p. 19):

> It opens with a heading naming the manor
> and the reeve or bailiff...and the period covered
> by the account, usually one year running from one
> Michaelmas (29 September) to the next. On the front
> [of the parchment membrane] are the cash receipts
> and payments, with cash balance; both are divided
> by subject-matter into a series of paragraphs, each
> with a marginal heading and a sub-total. On the
> dorse are first the corn, then the stock accounts;
> each category of corn or stock has a marginal
> heading and two paragraphs, one of receipts, one
> of expenditures, with a total following each and
> a concluding balance.

The entries on the dorse referred to quantities, not money values.
Surviving manorial accounts have markings that bear witness to
the thoroughness of their auditors' scrutiny. And it is likely
that an efficient auditor had a good enough understanding of
conversion ratios in agricultural activities to enable him to
challenge dubious entries.

Appendages to the stock account sometimes included a works
account, recording labour services due from tenants and rendered
by them, or a land account, listing the lands of the demesne and
their use during the accounting year.

Manorial accounts were often drawn up by clerks. The
reeve supplied the detailed information, partly from written records
if he were literate and partly from tallies; and "much may have
been stored in the astonishing memories which countryfolk develop
when the cannot write" (Plucknett, 1954, p. 6).

Other accounting documents used included manorial "extents".
These were detailed surveys of demesne lands and of tenants'
obligations, with the annual value "set on every piece of property
and every service" (Harvey, 1976, p. 75). An inventory of livestock
and equipment was often added to the manorial account when there
was a change of reeve. On larger estates household accounts were
also compiled at the centre, such as those kept in connection with
what Smith has called the *regimen scaccarii* in certain English
monasteries (Smith, 1947, p. 54).

Some manorial accounts after 1350 contain notes on the
manor's profits for the year. These notes rarely indicate the basis
of the profit calculation. Terms used for profit include *proficuum,*
clarum, and *valor.* According to E. Stone, such profit calculations
for Canterbury and Norwich cathedral priories influenced decisions
whether to lease particular manors or to run them in demesne. Stone
writes that these accounts of profit represent, in concept, "an
intellectual effort of an altogether higher order than that which
can be associated with the ordinary manorial account or with, say,
the older series of exchequer accounts" (Stone, 1962, p. 48).
P.D.A. Harvey suggests that the need to make economic decisions
on a better-informed basis may have been among the reasons for the
introduction of written manorial accounts (Harvey, 1976, pp. 56-7).

Reference to profit measurement leads naturally to the
accounts and accounting practices of medieval merchants, bankers,
and manufacturers, although often a calculation of profits was not
performed in their accounts.

Surviving medieval commercial accounting records are
diverse. They fall into two groups: accounts not kept on the
double-entry system, often unhelpfully lumped together as "single
entry"; and those kept on double-entry lines. A large number of
surviving European account-books up to 1500 are discussed in
Raymond de Roover's survey of 1956.

Early examples of accounting in business can be attributed
to credit transactions, or to relationships of accountability, or
to partnerships. The earliest surviving European business accounts
are fragments of an account-book dated 1211. The sheets record
in paragraph form details of loans made by an unknown firm of
bankers to customers (sometimes with the names of witnesses or
guarantors) and details of repayments. There are no totals nor
balances; the entries relating to a particular loan were crossed
through when it was fully repaid. Several other surviving medieval
account-books are likewise restricted to recording indebtedness
by and to the merchant.

The accounts of commercial agents or factors, sedentary
or itinerant, constitute another category of records. Some
account-books of factors employed by the commercial wing of the
Teutonic Knights have survived. Partnership enterprises also
generated accounts: in partnerships, credit relationships and
accountability relationships occur in combination. Parnters'
capital accounts were often included, showing what each partner
put into or drew out of the enterprise or was due from the enterprise.

Accounting records served other purposes as well. A cash account or cashbook provided some check on the cash or the cashier. Records of goods received and delivered helped control the warehouse keeper and gave information on stocks on hand. The monitoring of goods through accounts was especially important in the operation of the putting-out system in textile manufacturing (although the system worked even without written accounts). Finally, some account-books included classified information on particular kinds of incomes or expenses, or on particular trading ventures.

Accounting entries were arranged in various ways. The paragraph form of entry was probably the earliest. The account form presented information more clearly and accessibly: opposing types of entry (such as receipts and payments, creation and discharge of debt) were separated from each other, but those relating to a particular asset or person were united in a single "account". The "debit" and "credit" sections of an account were sometimes one above the other on the same ledger page, or were segregated in the two halves of the ledger. Eventually the bilateral form of ledger account came to prevail. A page was divided vertically into debit and credit sides; or the two pages of a ledger opening were given to debit and credit entries, respectively. In Italy the latter type of bilateral account was known as "alla Veneziana".

Profit calculations are found in many account-books not kept on the double-entry system (see, for example, Antoni, 1967, and de Roover, 1956, pp. 125, 128, 130, 172). From time to time assets were examined and listed, their values summed, and the amounts owing

to the creditors deducted; the difference between the current
and the preceding totals of the net assets was the profit for the
intervening period.

Account-books could have probatory value in law courts.
Their weight as evidence depended on circumstances: the position in
Italy is usefully summarised in Benvenuto Straccha, a mercantile
lawyer of Ancona, in *De Mercatura*, Venice, 1553. Merchants came to
have less need of notarised instruments. Sometimes the use of
account-books was regulated by a controlling authority. Thus the
statutes of the money-changers' gild in Florence (the *Arte del Cambio*)
included prohibition of the use of Arabic numerals in account-books,
because of the supposed ease of fraudulent alteration; provision
for the preservation by the gild of account-books of bankrupt
money-changers; and provision for the presentation of account-books
in cases of litigation. In Spain, account-books of private individuals
were dealt with in an enactment of Alfonso X in 1265. And the
Cuaderno de Alcabalas, enacted by Ferdinand and Isabella in 1491,
is of interest for its requirement that merchants keep account-books
and produce them to the tax authorities. The law did not specify
how the books or records were to be kept.

Today the double-entry method is overwhelminghly the
dominant accounting method. Its precise origins cannot be ascertained.
Suggestions that is was of Arabic or Indian origin lack supporting
evidence. Bearing in mind that there is a large element of chance
in the survival of records, and that the surviving records of early

enterprises tend to be incomplete, it is safest to locate the
origin of double entry - generally known throughout Europe until
the nineteenth century as the "Italian" method - in Italy (Genoa,
Florence, and Venice have had their champions), and to date it
toward the end of the thirteenth century.

It is not known whether the system emerged by a process of
slow evolution out of less complete systems, or whether a particular
individual or firm consciously pioneered the system and made it known
to others. Although it is sometimes claimed that "double entry
developed in response to the needs of nascent capitalism" (de Roover,
1956, p. 174), this explanation of its origins is unsatisfactory
because the particular needs, supposedly not met by other accounting
arrangements, are not distinctly specified.

But whatever the circumstances of its birth, by 1500
double entry was widely employed by Italian business enterprises.
There is evidence also of the use of the system by some non-business
organisations, including hospitals, monasteries, and communes.
The account-book of the *massari* of Genoa, dated 1340, was long
thought to be the earliest extant specimen of double entry. In 1494,
Luca Pacioli's *Summa de arithmetica* included the first published
exposition of the system. The claim that Pacioli plagiarized a
Venetian manuscript used in *scuole di abaco* may be true; but the
particular evidence adduced in its support is weak.

There is no convincing evidence that any non-Italian
merchant or banker kept his books by double entry before 1500.
Non-Italian businessmen or their bookkeepers could have acquired

a knowledge of the system in Italy or from Italian businessmen and
bookkeepers in their midst. Knowledge of doube entry was not
protected as an Italian trade secret.

The minimum requirements for accounts to qualify as
double entry are as follows (de Roover, 1956, p. 114):

> A necessary prerequisite is that all transactions
> be recorded twice, once on the debit and once on the
> the credit side [of the ledger]... This principle
> also involves the existence of an integrated system
> of accounts, both real [property, goods, debts] and
> nominal [incomes and expenses], so that the books
> will balance in the end, record changes in the
> owner's equity [capital] and permit the determination
> of profit or loss.

The system as described by Pacioli made use of three account-books:
the memorial, in which transactions were noted chronologically by
whomever was involved; the journal, in which the transactions were
transcribed chronologically in proper form, with the debit and
credit elements clearly identified; and the ledger, in which the
information in the journal was entered in the appropriate debit
and credit sections of the relevant accounts.

In practice arrangements were usually more elaborate, with,
say, the ledger sub-divided to facilitate the bookkeeping operations
of large firms or of complex businesses. Thus there could be
separate ledgers for different groups of debtors or creditors.
Many of the larger firms had secret ledgers, reserved for the
partners' accounts and other sensitive accounts. The variety and
degree of sub-division of ledger accounts also varied according to

circumstances.   Voyage accounts featured prominently in Venetian

mercantile ledgers.   In the ledgers of Tuscan textile manufacturing

concerns, separate accounts for each process permitted the

accounting control of the flow of materials.

The double-entry system was more comprehensive in scope

than alternative methods.   Further, it had the potential to

organise information systematically; it provided for a check on

the arithmetical accuracy of the ledger; and it permitted the

production of summary accounts: the profit-and-loss account and

the balance account, containing the balances on asset, liability,

and capital accounts.

Did the introduction of double entry improve business

organisation and administration, and entrepreneurial decisions?

Order, clarity, and accuracy in accounts evidently were useful.

But these features could not be guaranteed by double entry itself.

For example, eight of the ten published fifteenth century balance

accounts of the Medici bank do not balance, an indication that

errors in the ledger were not tracked down and corrected, as

Pacioli was to specify should be done.   Further, comprehensiveness

in business recording was an advantage, but was achieved at the

cost of clerical effort.

It has been argued that double entry made possible or

materially facilitated the development of sedentary trading, the

use of agents or factors, the operation of partnerships or companies,

and even the development of banking.   Such claims for double entry

are amply refuted by the historical record and by simple consideration

of the relevant business needs (Yamey, 1975).

More generally, the view is sometimes expressed that double-entry bookkeeping was one of the various business techniques developed and used in Italy that help to explain why medieval Italian business enterprises were more efficient than their counterparts in the rest of Europe. This view has been challenged on various grounds. The fact or extent of the superiority of Italian accounting techniques has been questioned (for instance, by Blockmans and Lopez, in the conference volume *Finances et Comptabilité Urbaines*, 1964, pp. 217-218). Moreover, the Datini, Bardi, Peruzzi, Alberti, and Medici enterprises in Italy cannot be shown to have been less efficiently run before they had adopted double entry in their accounting than after they did so. And the German Welser and Fugger family firms operated large dispersed enterprises in the fifteenth century without having double-entry records. Apparently they and others like them did not introduce the Italian system, although it must have been accessible to them.

Caution is necessary, therefore, when appraising even more sweeping and more general historical claims for the double-entry system and for its introduction, such as those made by the German historian, Werner Sombart. He asserted that "capitalism without double-entry bookkeeping is simply inconceivable. They hold together as form and matter"; and that "with this [double-entry] way of thinking the concept of capital is first created" (Sombart, 1924, pp. 118-120). More recently Federigo Melis wrote: "...It is capitalism which begets the method [double-entry], creating the necessary conditions for its existence; and it is capitalism, on

the other hand, which requires this perfect instrument to attain
its objectives" (Melis, 1950, p. 598).

Sombart's more detailed discussion of the inter-connections
between capitalism and double entry - that of Melis is short and
general - is interesting, but not persuasive. Among other
considerations, one may note that it is difficult to discern any
systematic relationship between the mentality of businessmen and
their accounting methods and practices; that Sombart was wrong in
supposing that the "rationalistic" pursuit of profits or effective
decision-making depended upon systematic calculation of past
profits, notably so when markets were volatile and communications
slow; that, in so far as profit figures might have been relevant
for rational decision-making, double entry was not essential for
their production; that the concepts and accounting quantification
of profits and capital preceded the adoption of double entry; and
that the recognition of the firm as an entity distinct from its
owners did not depend upon double-entry accounting or have the
far-reaching consequences attributed to it by Sombart.

Double-entry bookkeeping or accounting is an intellectually
satisfying and interesting achievement of medieval Italian business.
It had real but nevertheless modest practical utility.

BIBLIOGRAPHY

[Most of the items listed include references to sources, published
documents and secondary materials.]

Antoni, T, *Il Libro dei Bilanci di una Azienda Mercantile del
Trecento*, Pisa,1967.

Astuti, G. and F. Melis, "L'Esplorazione dei Fondi storico-economici
dell'Archivio di S. Pietro di Perugia", *Benedictina*, 6, 1952 ,
309-17.

Brambilla, G., *Storia della Ragioneria Italiana*, Milan, 1901, ch.2.

Clanchy, M.T., *From Memory to Written Record: England 1066-1307*,
London, 1979.

Dölger, F., *Beiträge zur Geschichte der byzantinischen Finanzverwaltung
besonders des 10 und 11 Jahrhunderts*, Hildesheim, 1960, 92-112.

Favier, J., *Les Finances Pontificales a L'Epoque du Grand Schism
D'Occident 1379-1409*, Paris, 1966, 41-135.

Finances et Comptabilité Urbaines du XIIIe au XVIe Siècle: Actes,
Brussels, 1964.

Ganshof, L., *Frankish Institutions under Charlemagne*, Providence, R.I.,
1968, 34-35.

Harvey, P.D.A., (ed.), *Manorial Records of Cuxham, Oxfordshire, circa
1200-1359*, London, 1976.

────── "Agricultural Treatises on Manorial Accounting In England",
Agricultural History, 20, 1972, 178-179.

Haskins, C.H.,"England and Sicily in the Twelfth Century", *English
Historical Review*, 26, 1911, 651-655.

Henneman, J.B., *Royal Taxation in Fourteenth Century France*, Princeton,
N.J., 1971, appendix 1.

Hernandez Esteve, E., "Legislacion Castellana de la Baja Edad Media
y Comienzos del Renacimiento sobre Contabilidad y Libros
de Cuentas de Mercaderes", paper presented at Journées
Internationales d'Histoire du Droit, Valladolid, June 1981.

Johnson, C., *The Course of the Exchequer, by Richard, son of Nigel*,
London, 1950.

Lee, G., "The Oldest European Account Book: a Florentine Bank Ledger
of 1211", *Nottingham Mediaeval Studies*, 16, 1972, 28-60.

—— "The Development of Italian Bookkeeping 1211-1300", *Abacus: A Journal of Accounting and Business Studies*, 9, 1973, 137-155.

Lunt, E., *Papal Revenues in the Middle Ages*, New York, 1934, vol.1, 3-51.

Lyon, B. and A. Verhulst, *Medieval Finance: A Comparison of Financial Institutions in North-Western Europe*, Bruges, 1967.

Martin, G.H., "The English Borough in the Thirteenth Century", *Transactions of the Royal Historical Society*, 5th Ser., 13, 1963, 123-144.

Melis, F., *Storia della Ragioneria*, Bologna, 1950, 381-602.

—— *Aspetti della Vita Economica Medievale (Studi nell'Archivio Datini di Prato)*, Florence, 1962, part 4.

—— *Documenti per la Storia Economica dei Secoli XIII-XVI*, Florence, 1972, 49-74, 377-462.

Metz, W., *Das karolingische Reichsgut: Eine verfassungs- und verwaltungsgeschichtliche Untersuchung*, Berlin, 1960, 18-25, 77-87.

Nokes, C., "Accounting for Bailiffship in Thirteenth Century England", *Accounting and Business Research*, Spring, 1981.

Nortier, M. and J.W. Baldwin, "Contributions a l'Etude des Finances de Philippe Auguste", *Biblioteque de l'Ecole des Chartes*, 138, 1980, 5-33.

Oschinsky, D., *Walter of Henley and other Treatises on Estate Management and Accounting*, Oxford, 1971.

Partner, P., "The 'Budget' of the Roman Church in the Renaissance Period", in E.F. Jacob (ed.), *Italian Renaissance Studies*, London, 1960, 256-278.

Patze, H., "Neue Typen des Geschäftsschriftgutes im 14. Jahrhundert", in H. Patze (ed.), *Der Deutsche Territorialstaat im 14. Jahrhundert*, Sigmaringen, 1970, vol.1, 48-53.

Penndorf, B., *Geschichte der Buchhaltung in Deutschland*, Leipzig, 1913, 3-36.

Plucknett, T.F.T., *The Mediaeval Bailiff*, London, 1954.

Poole, R.L., *The Exchequer in the Twelfth Century*, Oxford, 1912.

de Roover, R., "New Perspectives on the History of Accounting",
    Accounting Review, 30, 1955, 405-420.

───── "The Development of Accounting Prior to Luca Pacioli according
    to the Account-books of Medieval Merchants", in A.C. Littleton
    and B.S. Yamey (eds.), *Studies in the History of Accounting*,
    London, 1956, 114-174; reprinted in his *Business, Banking
    and Economic Thought in Late Medieval and Early Modern
    Europe*, ed. J. Kirshner, Chicago, 1974, 119-180.

───── *The Rise and Decline of the Medici Bank 1397-1494*, Cambridge,
    Mass., 1963.

de Ste Croix, G.E.M., "Greek and Roman Accounting", in Littleton
    and Yamey (eds.), *op.cit.*, 14-74.

Schubert, E., *König und Reich: Studien zur Spätmittelalterlichen
    deutschen Verfassungsgeschichte*, Gottingen, 1979, 147-150.

Smith, R.A.L., "The *Regimen Scaccarii* in English Monasteries", in
    his *Collected Papers*, London, 1947, 54-73.

Sombart, W., *Der moderne Kapitalismus*, Munich, 1924, vol.2, 110-125.

Stone, E., "Profit-and-Loss Accountancy at Norwich Cathedral Priory",
    Transactions of the Royal Historical Society, 5th ser.,
    12, 1962, 25-48.

Strayer, J.R., *The Administration of Normandy under Saint Louis*,
    Cambridge, Mass., 1932, 32-55.

von Stromer, W., "Das Schriftwesen der Nürnberger Wirtschaft vom
    14. bis zum 16. Jahrhundert: Zur Geschichte Oberdeutscher
    Handelsbücher", *Beiträge zur Wirtschaftsgeschichte Nürnbergs*,
    2, 1967, 752-799.

Thielen, P.G., *Der Verwaltung des Ordensstaates Preussen vornehmlich
    im 15. Jahrhundert*, Cologne, 1965.

Yamey, B.S., "Accounting and the Rise of Capitalism: Further Notes
    on a Theme by Sombart", *Journal of Accounting Research*, 2
    1964, 117-136; reprinted in his *Essays on the History of
    Accounting*, New York, 1978.

───── "Notes on Double-Entry Bookkeeping and Economic Progress",
    Journal of European Economic History, 4, 1975, 717-723;
    reprinted in his *Essays, op.cit.*

Zerbi, T., *Le Origini della Partita Doppia*, Milan, 1952.

EARLY VIEWS ON THE ORIGINS AND
DEVELOPMENT OF BOOKKEEPING
AND ACCOUNTING

Early Views on the Origins and Development of Book-keeping and Accounting

B. S. Yamey

Introduction

'The origin of Book-keeping is involved in much doubt...', wrote F. Hayne Carter in 1861; and he added: '...up to the present time, the inquisitive, or rather curious in such matters, have merely indulged in conjectures'. He was basically correct. Those who had written on the history of book-keeping generally, or on the history of the double-entry system more specifically, had rarely examined surviving records. Instead, there was speculation on the nature of the commercial environment in which, it was argued or implied, certain developments must necessarily have taken place. The changing requirements of merchants, it was posited, must have induced improvements or changes in commercial recording and accounting. There was also speculation whether developments outside the commercial field would have had an impact on developments in book-keeping and accounts. In this context the invention of writing, the introduction of Arabic numerals and of the decimal system, and the diffusion of knowledge of algebra all received some attention, however slight. Nevertheless, one source of historical information was made use of, if only superficially. References to earlier published treatises on book-keeping are not infrequent. But these references rarely relate to the book-keeping or accounting practices or procedures described or advocated in these earlier books. Further, both the fruits of speculation and also references to treatises were quite often taken by one writer from another, sometimes with acknowledgement and sometimes without. Demonstrable errors were sometimes transmitted from one author to another.

In this article I review early contributions (up to about 1860) to the study of the history of book-keeping and accounting. Almost all the contribu-

tors were themselves authors of treatises on book-keeping.

The review is not intended to be exhaustive. Comment is limited to points of information, since little purpose would be served by commenting on early views in the light of research done by scholars and enthusiasts in more recent decades into 'the musty records of bygone trading communities'[1] and the treatises on book-keeping and accounts.

Early treatises as historical sources

Before we come to those authors who deliberately addressed themselves to the subject of the history of book-keeping and accounting, we should note that many authors of early book-keeping treatises give isolated pieces of information which are of some interest to those who today concern themselves with the history of the subject. Some examples of this scattered material follow, arranged in three groups for convenience.

First, there are observations or comments which tell us something about contemporary practices or conditions. Thus Pacioli (1494) remarks that in his exposition of double-entry book-keeping he would be using the method employed in Venice (el modo di Vinegia), which was certainly to be recommended above all other methods and knowledge of which enabled one to understand the others. This tells us several things, such as that Pacioli did not claim to invent double entry (as is still sometimes said) and that the style of entries and arrangement of accounts

---

[1] '...Were its [the origin of book-keeping's] elucidation of any importance, there would be no lack of enthusiasts to make researches into the musty records of bygone trading communities...'. Carter (1861).

differed from one place to another. Pacioli also described the authentication of account-books in Perugia; and, in the same chapter, says that some keep two sets of their books, one to show to customers and the other to suppliers.

Some passages in Peele (1569) suggest that at an early date those skilled in accounts were called in by merchants to clear up sets of accounts which had fallen into disarray or to settle disputes arising out of accounts. In the introductory 'dialogue between the marchante & the scholemaster', the merchant receives an affirmative answer to the question: 'Was it not you that passed thaccompte betwene Marten. I. and Thomas. B. uppon the matter so longe in question betwene them?' The schoolmaster answers affirmatively, and adds: '...and I thanke God it is the leaste of a nombre of things that I have brought from depe doubte to perfecte lighte, as theye knowe who have tasted of my travell [travail], to their profit I truste.'

De Renterghem (1592) indicates that some of his countrymen in the Low Countries went abroad to study business practice. With the publication of his book on book-keeping, however, such excursions would no longer be necessary. Merchants, apprentices, factors and cashiers could acquire the necessary knowledge at home on their chairs, without discomfort or cost, solely for the price to be paid for the author's industry and effort.[2] Dafforne (1635), on his return to his native England after several years in Holland, notes the paucity of good books on book-keeping in the English language. He explains this in part in terms of the neglect by the English merchants of domestic publications and the 'small love...that a great part of our Merchants beare to this Science'. Hence, 'how then shall our Youth attaine unto this Art, but by frequenting abroad amongst other Nations?' If English authors were encouraged at home ('....by Love allure, and with Reward induce...'), 'our Youth should not need to bee transported into other Countries for Arts Documents'.

Jan Ympyn, a Flemish merchant who had travelled widely, in his book (1543) praises the Spanish merchants for the neatness of the entries in their account-books, and also the Germans who had learnt from the Italians. He was critical of the merchants of the Low Countries, France and England, where even those with large businesses did not keep their accounts by the double-entry method described in his book.

As to specific book-keeping practices, something can be gleaned from incidental comments. Thus a remark by Stevin (1607) suggests that, at least in the Low Countries, the use of compound journal entries was unusual. Moschetti (1610), who writes in the Venetian tradition, describes three different ways of closing a ledger and opening its successor, and in his illustrative example demonstrates yet another method. This suggests that a variety of methods was to be found in practice. Leuchs claims in his book (1806) that he had invented the breaking-up of the comprehensive book of original entry into a number of specialised books, one for each category of transaction.[3] He was wrong, as the 'invention' in the literature goes back to Weddington (1567), and in practice before then. But his claim suggests, at least, that the use of specialised books of original entry was limited in Germany in the early 1800s.

Second, several of the authors refer, usually at the beginning of their texts, to some of their predecessors, sometimes with comments on their treatises. Such lists or references can be of interest in various ways. For example, early references to Ympyn (1543) suggest that those who came after him did not doubt that he was the author of the book, despite what he seems to have said in his preface.[4] Thus Mellema (1590) observes that 'Ympyn's 'Book-keeper' is highly praised by many; yet the following are better' (and he names three). And de Renterghem (1592) writes that 'several attribute very much to Jean Ympyn'. Again, the German Gammersfelder (1570) writes that Ympyn had given a 'very fine description of the Italian book-keeping system in the Netherlandish language'.[5] Another example concerns Pacioli, author of the first published exposition of book-keeping (1494). His name is not mentioned by Manzoni (1540), whose text is Paciolian; but it is by Ympyn (1543). It is among the names referred to by Flori (1636), but not by Moschetti (1610). The patchy recognition of Pacioli by his successors remains a puzzle. Yet another example of what can be derived from early authors is the

---

[2]See de Waal (1927), pp. 222–3.

[3]See Penndorf (1913), p. 202.

[4]On this question, see 'The Authorship and Sources of the 'Nieuwe Instructie' ', in Yamey (1978).

[5]See Penndorf (1913), p. 141.

In the introduction to Pietersz (1583) the author claims to be the first writer on book-keeping in the Dutch language. He either did not know Ympyn's work, or he concealed his knowledge. He also writes that the Italian book-keeping system was not commonly used at the time he was writing. See de Waal (1927), p. 159.

inclusion in some lists of the name of Forestain (or variants of it). The name appears in Mellema (1590), Dafforne (1635) and Geestevelt's edition of Kock (1658).[6] Presumably Forestain had compiled a manuscript or had published a book which has since completely disappeared.

It is worth digressing to note why some of the authors gave their lists of predecessors. Mellema (1590) includes his long list and commentary to honour those whom he knew in person or through their works. De Renterghem (1592) concludes his list with the remark that the publication of his own book is not misplaced: even the deeds of Alexander the Great did not prevent those who came after him from achieving many great and useful things.[7] Irson (1687) has a list of authors who had written in French. He says of them: 'I greatly venerate those who have preceded me, they achieved much; but they did not reach the Pillars of Hercules; much remains to be done'.

Third, some of the early authors made brief observations relating to the origins of accounting or of the double-entry system. Thus Peele (1569) in his preface answers as follows those who prefer 'their owne orders [methods]' to the double-entry system he sets forth:

It is probable enoughe that this order is both auncient and famous: and doubtles grounded altogether uppon reason, for tyme oute of mynde, it hath bene and is frequented, by divers nacions, and chiefelye by suche as have bene and be the most auncient and famous Merchauntes. The firste invencion whereof, semethe to growe of an ernest desier, instantlye to make playne and manifest (withoute prolonginge of tyme) that, whiche otherwyse wold be darke and obscure, seasinge presentlye thereby all suspicion...

Gammersfelder (1570) refers to the long history of the Italian system when he is rebutting the charge of some of his detractors who doubtlessly would say that his book-keeping 'was an old book-keeping'. He says that he cannot ascribe the invention of the Italian system to any of his author predecessors (such as Schweicker [1549] or Ympyn [1543]), because the system had been

in use for many centuries (*viel Hundert Jar*) by the Italians. And no one can claim to invent a new kind or system ('Art') of Italian book-keeping, since each must adhere to the old practice and to the rules that go with it.[8]

Anderson and Beckmann, two general historians

We turn now to more deliberate treatments of the history of book-keeping. The presentation here is largely in chronological order of publication.

Hager (1660) expresses the view that the origination and invention of book-keeping are to be attributed primarily to the Egyptians who were 'most acute inventors of difficult and almost unfathomable things, and who never missed an opportunity to sharpen their mental faculties'. From them the knowledge went to the Greeks who, according to Pliny and others, conducted large and impressive trading operations. Italy inherited the science from the Greeks, after the fall of Troy, Tyre and Sidon etc; and, eventually, through daily business contact, it came to his (Hager's) fatherland, Germany. He explains that the double-entry system originally came to Germany from Italy. But in the leading German cities the system was purified and brought to perfection, the original Italian practice having evidently been rather obscure and inconvenient (*rauch undt unbequemd*). In Germany the system was perfected after much effort, so that it was no longer reasonable to call it the 'Italian' system.

Gordon (1765) is more expansive on the historical origins and diffusion of accounting, extending his discussion over three paragraphs. He speculates broadly on the early history and presents a reconstruction of what he thought must necessarily have happened:

In the earlier ages of the world, when all accounts were settled by barter on the spot, there was little occasion for accountantship; but by degrees, as invention grew upon experience, conveniencies of life formerly unknown were produced, and mankind, emulous to excel, gave genius and industry full scope: thus was the use of money, weights, measures, navigation, arts, manufactures, laws, government, credit, correspondence, banks, bills of exchange, &c. introduced and established, and consequently the use of accountantship became obvious and indispensable. It was not, however, carried to its greatest perfection at once;

---

[6]On Forestain, see Yamey (1967), pp. 72–3; reprinted in Yamey (1978) with 'Additional Notes', p. 9.

[7]On the strength of their lists and commentaries, Stevelinck says that Mellema and de Renterghem 'take their place among the first historians of accounting to whom present-day historians are greatly indebted'. Stevelinck (1970), p. 78.

[8]See Penndorf (1913), p. 141.

without doubt, as commerce flourished, and credit became more extensive, the method of arranging and adjusting accounts, became likewise by degrees more regular and uniform.

Were we to trace this important science back to its original, we would be naturally led to ascribe the first invention to the first considerable merchants; and there are none who have a fairer claim to precedency in point of time than those of Arabia. The Egyptians, who for many ages made a glorious appearance in the commercial world, derived their first notions of trade from their intercourse with these ingenious people; and, of consequence, from them likewise they must have received their first form of accountantship, which, in the natural way of trade, was communicated to all the cities on the Mediterranean. When the western empire had been over-run by the Barbarians, and all the countries of which it had been composed, took that opportunity of asserting their own independency, commerce fled quickly after liberty; and immediately Italy, which had formerly been the court of the universe, became the seat of trade; to which the ruin of the eastern empire by the Turks, into whose genius or constitution the arts of commerce never entered, did not a little contribute. The business of exchange, by which the Lombards connected all the trading cities of Europe, likewise introduced their method of keeping accounts, by double entry; whence, at this day, it gets the name of Italian book-keeping.

Thus was the knowledge of accountantship diffused, not only throughout Europe, but by degrees through all the trading-countries in the world; by which means a happy regularity and uniformity in accounts every where prevailed, public and private credit were extended, correspondence was enlarged, and property ascertained, not only among merchants, but all other ranks and degrees of men, from the public revenue to the meanest private business...

And he ends his short history with resounding praise for the art (and some may be willing with the exercise of imagination to read into it a prophetic reference to national income accounting): 'For such is the peculiar. excellency of this art, that the accounts of nations can be as easily adjusted thereby, as those of a merchant, it being as readily applied to millions, as hundreds of pounds'.

Simon Stevin (1548–1620), tutor, counsellor and

friend of Prince Maurice of Nassau, was a distinguished polymath—mathematician, natural philosopher, physicist, engineer and financial expert. In his writings on book-keeping and accounts, written in Dutch in the early years of the seventeenth century and translated into French and Latin, he included an 'Opinion of Book-keepings Antiquity' (to quote the translation in Dafforne (1635)). Stevin relates how a good friend of his, who had seen his (Stevin's) own work before it was published, and who 'was exercised in the old Histories', expressed the view that the double-entry system had not only been in use in Italy for the last two centuries, as some believed, but that the same 'forme' or 'one in many parts very like this, was used in the time of Julius Caesar, and in Rome long before'. He conjectured that 'some Reliques of Ancient time are come into the hands of them, that of late have revived it [the system] againe'.

These conjectures seemed reasonable and appealed to Stevin, who found it strange to suppose that this glorious recondite art could have been invented during the *barbari soeculi*. He therefore reproduces the evidence given by his friend, namely that terms found 'in innumerable places of the Latin Writers, but especially *ex Oratione Ciceronis pro Roscio Comoedo*' evidently had the same meanings as those of terms used in the double-entry system. Stevin comments that further enquiries might show that the Romans acquired the art from the Greeks. The Romans 'were no great Inventors', and derived their knowledge of the arts in large measure from the Greeks.

This short statement in Stevin was translated into English in Dafforne (1635), and the original was paraphrased in part in van Gezel (1681). Its contents were to reappear in several later discussions of the history of accounting.[9]

In his *Historical ... deduction of the Origin of Commerce* (1764) Anderson refers to the conjectures expressed in Stevin.[10] He had consulted the French version of Stevin, the 'ingenious and judicious Simon Stevin of Bruges'. He reproduces the main points; and on the view that the Romans inherited double-entry book-keeping from the

---

[9]The authoritative modern discussion of Greek and Roman accounting records is G. E. M. de Ste Croix, 'Greek and Roman Accounting', in Littleton and Yamey (eds.) (1956), pp. 14–74.

[10]Anderson's discussion of book-keeping and accounts is in Anderson (1764), vol. 1, pp. 318, 408–9.

Greeks, he writes: 'Be that as it may, we must surely admit this to be a very curious Piece of History and mercantile Criticism'. Anderson's own inclination appears to have been in favour of a different origin. After some speculation on the origins of algebra, he writes:

What is more to our present Purpose, is the great Probability that the algebraic Art proved the Introduction of the Art of Merchants Accounts by Double Entry, commonly called Italian Book-keeping, the latter being grounded on the principles of the former...

And later:

In all Probability, this Art of Double-Entry Accounts had its Rise (or at least its Revival) amongst the mercantile Cities of Italy; possibly it might be first known at Venice, about the Time that numeral Algebra was taught there, from the Principles of which Science Double-Entry, or what we call Merchants-Accounts seems to have been deduced, viz. about the Middle of the XVth Century, though it did not reach England until its Commerce (about this Time) [i.e. the sixteenth century] began to be considerable.

And he then refers to the fact that the 'earliest printed Author on it [i.e. algebra] was one Lucas de Burgo [i.e. Luca Pacioli], an Italian Friar'.

It is convenient again to depart from strict chronological order and to consider briefly David Macpherson's Annals (1805), since much of it was acknowledged to be based on Anderson.[11] On the antiquity of the double-entry system Macpherson expresses two contrary and apparently irreconcilable views. First,

If I am right in my opinion (which seems supported by good authority), that book-keeping by double entry was known to the Romans, it may be presumed that some knowledge of it was kept up through all the darkness of the middle ages in Italy; and thence it has got the name of Italian book-keeping.

Second:

I believe there is nothing extant, which can inform us whether they [the Romans] raised

accounts for the several articles of merchandize in their books, or whether every transaction was entered in two accounts; or, in other words, whether they understood any thing of double entry.

As to the origins of book-keeping generally, and not the double-entry system itself, Macpherson writes:

As book-keeping is an art so essentially necessary to commerce, and so simple in its principles, it cannot be supposed that the Phoenecians, or indeed any nation carrying on trade, and understanding arithmetic, could be destitute of it. With the Phoenecian colonies it may have spread into Rhodes, Crete, Thebes in Greece, and other places, where they mixed with the Greeks; and from the Greeks, it is most possible, that the Romans received it along with other branches of their knowledge.

Johann Beckmann's multi-volume work on the history of inventions (1783) has as its very first section the subject 'of Italian Book-keeping'.[12] Beckmann, who was professor of economics (Professor der Oekonomie) at the University of Göttingen, and a Hofrath, was a prolific author. He published a short book on book-keeping in 1797.[13]

Beckmann, in this respect like Hager, notes that the use of the description 'Italian book-keeping' and the many words of Italian origin used in the practice of book-keeping in all languages, point to the high probability that double entry was invented by the Italians. Other peoples acquired

---

[11]See Macpherson (1805), vol. 1, Preface. The discussion of book-keeping is in vol. 1, pp. 145–6, and vol. 2, p. 149.

[12]Beckmann (1783), vol. 1 of the 'second and somewhat improved edition', pp. 1–15. An addendum is in section 2 of the second part of the second volume (dated 1785), pp. 177–85. In Johnston's English translation (2nd ed., 1814) of Beckmann material in the two sections is combined, with some omissions: vol. 1, pp. 1–9.

[13]In this book Beckmann explains that after he had given his lectures on mercantile science, including merchants' double-entry book-keeping, he was asked whether double entry was adaptable for the use of various types of entity, including small households (kleine Haushaltungen). He says the system was not suitable for such concerns, and he could find no published work which set out a satisfactory method for the purpose. He therefore wrote his book, and in it adopted some of the ideas of a short anonymous work published in Berlin in 1786, but difficult to obtain. The book is a combination of advice on managing the household's finances and on accounting. Among the various observations is the following: 'It is true that it is repugnant, melancholic and unpleasant to examine a ledger of one's debts; but of what use is it if a soldier closes his eyes when taking aim?

their knowledge of it, as well as of various innovations in commercial arithmetic, from the Italians, at the time when all the trade with the East passed through Italy. Basing himself on an observation in de la Porte (1753), and on Anderson's reference to Lucas de Burgo, Beckmann concludes that the latter was the first writer on the subject of double-entry book-keeping, in his book of 1494.[14]

He then takes up Anderson's statement that Peele's book of 1569 was the earliest publication on the subject printed in England. After doubting whether one could be satisfied from the few details given by Anderson that Peele was dealing with double entry, he goes on to establish, by way of an entry in Ames' *Typographical Antiquities* (1749), that a book by Hugh Oldcastle, evidently on the double-entry system, had been published in 1543, and re-issued by Mellis in 1588.

Beckmann goes on to claim that Gottlieb's book of 1531, which he was able to study in his university library, was the earliest book published in German. He drew this conclusion, which is not correct, from the fact that Gottlieb writes that no exposition as comprehensible and clear (*so Teutsch verstendig und unvertunckelt*) as his had ever before been printed. This statement, however, is compatible with the existence of earlier publications; and Schreiber's exposition had in fact been published in 1518. Beckmann discusses the contents of Gottlieb at some length to establish that it does describe the double-entry system. From another statement by Gottlieb to the effect that he knew of some 40 variants of the system, Beckmann infers that the system itself must have been widely practised in Germany at the time.

Beckmann also refers to Anderson's short discussion of Simon Stevin's advice to Prince Maurice of Nassau that the accounts of the public finances should be kept on mercantile double-entry lines. He comments: 'It is noteworthy, in truth, that already by the end of the sixteenth century someone had the notion to apply the merchants' method of keeping accounts to the public finances or public accounts' (*beym Kammerwesen oder bey den Cameralrechnungen anzuwenden*). He regrets that he could not probe further into this matter because he did not have access to Stevin's work. (In a later addendum to the substantive section, Beckmann reports that he had subsequently been able to examine Stevin's work. He notes that Stevin stated expressly that in 1604 Prince Maurice had employed a competent bookkeeper to adapt the treasury accounts to the Italian system, with excellent results. He was unable to ascertain, however, how long this innovation was continued.)[15] He returns to the subject at the end of the section. He notes that attempts had been made in Vienna to improve public accounting by the application of double entry. He refers to the authors of several publications, mostly expensive, for information about this. Recalling Stevin, he says that the claim made by some to the effect that Count Zinzendorf was the author and patron of that admirable invention, the application of double entry to the public finances, should be somewhat diminished.

Beckmann's survey also takes in Stevin on the Roman origins of double entry. He is sceptical:

>... it is unproven and improbable, in my opinion, that they [the Romans] would have known the rather sophisticated [*weit künstlichere*] double-entry book-keeping with the various accounts for assets, ventures etc., together with the arrangement by which the accounts are balanced through the balance account....

And he goes on to explain that the business affairs of merchants in ancient times were not so complicated and multifarious as to have required such

---

[14]Beckmann gives the correct date of 1494, although in de la Porte (1753) it is given as *vers l'an 1495*. This incorrect date appears in several later publications, following de la Porte. See for example Kelly (1801) in the text below. See also Boucher (1803), who alters his unacknowledged model to state that *frère Luc* (Pacioli) invented double entry.

Boucher is interesting on public accounting. He notes that Colbert had hoped to introduce the double-entry system in the public accounts, but that, quoting Barrême (1721) not altogether accurately, the project was abandoned because *ce ministre ne trouva point de sujets qui pussent soumettre l'ordre des parties doubles à l'ancien ordre et à la manière de compter à la chambre.* Boucher asks what obstacle stands in the way of the introduction of double entry into the public accounts:

> Est-elle moins compliquée que celles des Hopes d'Amsterdam, et des Popes et Chapeaurouge de Hambourg? ou est-elle plus compliquée que toutes celles d'Europe ensemble? Dans le premier cas, son admission ne peut nullement souffrir de difficulté, puisque même de petits négocians s'en servent; dans le second cas, elle est absolument des plus utiles, puisqu'elle a la propriété de classer les idées les plus ramifiées, et que la preuve est toujours à côté du fait.

---

[15]This statement is in the addendum in Beckmann.

Anderson's comment on Prince Maurice's introduction of double entry is as follows: 'If Prince Maurice practised this Art, with respect to all his Principalities, Domains and Finances, it is not improbable, that he was the first Sovereign Prince that ever did, and possibly the last that ever will descend to so frugal (or Merchant-like) a Piece of Oeconomy'. Some authors give examples of deficiencies in public accounts; for example, North (1714).

an analytical system of accounting. They did not have bills of exchange or insurances.

The views of accounting authors, 1801–1833

In 1801 the writers of two treatises on book-keeping included fairly lengthy accounts of the history of their subject.

Dr. Patrick Kelly's popular treatise, *The Elements of Book-keeping* (first ed. 1801), went into 12 editions in the first half of the nineteenth century. He was a celebrated mathematician and astronomer.[16]

His textbook includes in the preface a 6-page 'A Short History of Book-keeping'.[17] This begins with the statement that 'the origin of Book-keeping, like that of most other useful arts, is involved in great obscurity'. He writes that 'it is generally supposed to have been first practised at Venice, in the fifteenth century, when that city was the grand Emporium of Europe'. He evidently had the double-entry system in mind;[18] for he goes on to address himself to Stevin's view that 'Double Entry was known to the Ancients, and revived only in Italy with the revival of commerce'. Of the evidence that the Ancients 'entered the receipts and payments of money on opposite pages, in the way of Debtor and Creditor', he observes that 'nothing beyond Single Entry can be inferred from this practice'. And he goes on to say that it is improbable that anything more than single entry 'was wanted in the rude and simple state of ancient commerce':

> Insurances, Bills of Exchange, and other modern improvements, demanded, and, in all probability, produced, correspondent improvements in the mode of keeping Accounts; but that which places the subject in the clearest light is, that none of the technical terms of Double Entry are to be found in the ancient languages, but appear immediately derived from the Italian, as adopted in the other languages of Europe.

In a footnote the author adds that the Jews, 'as they were the principal Merchants of Italy, when Italian Book-keeping was first used, it may be fairly presumed that they had also some share in this invention'. He notes that Savary had recorded in his *Dictionnaire* that the Jews 'first practised Insurance; and the invention of Bills of Exchange is universally ascribed to this commercial people'.

As to the nature of double-entry book-keeping, this 'too admits of various conjectures with respect to its origin':

> The double purpose of a Bill of Exchange, and the manner of recording the same, might have very naturally suggested the idea of Double Entry; the principle might have been even deduced from the Axioms of Euclid, or the properties of an Algebraic Equation; and the first European who translated Algebra from the writings of the Arabians, is also supposed to have written the first Treatise of Book-keeping. It was published in the Italian language at Venice, about the year 1495, by Lucas de Burgo, a Friar, who likewise wrote several useful works on Mathematical subjects.

The remainder of Kelly's essay is taken up with references to earlier works on book-keeping in the English language, including those of Oldcastle and Peele. He mentions several later authors, notes that all of them 'were either Schoolmasters or Teachers', and praises the book (1789) by Benjamin Booth, 'a Merchant', on which he himself drew. Finally, he comes to Jones's *English Book-keeping* (1796), 'a work chiefly remarkable for the enormous subscription raised on the occasion'. The work, however, 'did not answer the expectations of the public'. Nevertheless,

> Some of the columns have been adopted in Counting-houses and even by subsequent Writers, and the publication has, besides, given rise to much useful enquiry and investigation on the subject of Merchants Accounts.

Andreas Wagner, described as professor in a commercial academy in Magdeburg, published his first work in 1801. This includes an 8-page history of book-keeping systems.[19]

---

[16]Woolf (1913), p. 142.

[17]This material is used in Rees (1819), with proper acknowledgement. I owe this reference to Dr. K. Nishikawa.

[18]Venice, as the major commercial centre of Early Modern Europe, has often been seen as the birthplace of double entry. The noted orientalist, Alexander Hamilton (1798) thought that Venice was the system's port of entry into Europe, but that it was imported from the Banians of India: 'We would remark that the Banians of India have been, from time immemorial, in possession of the method of book-keeping by double-entry, and that Venice was the emporium of Indian commerce at the time at which Friar Lucas's treatise appeared'.

[19]Much of this material is repeated, with acknowledgement, in Buse (1804). Buse also uses material from Anderson and Beckmann, duly acknowledged. Isler (1810) has a short section *Sur L'Origine de la Tenue des Livres en Partie Double*. Most of this is taken without acknowledgement from Wagner. A few points not in Wagner are reminiscent of Gordon (1765). The section *Geschichte der Entstehung der Italienischen Buchhalten* in Grimm (1828) is plagiarised from Wagner.

This history begins as follows (reminiscent of Gordon): 'When commerce was still in its infancy and consisted of barter of food and goods, there was far from being any need to write and record in any way the transactions that occurred'. Barter took place long before the invention of writing. The invention of writing marked a new epoch in commerce. It is highly probable that mercantile business was one of the most powerful driving forces which gave rise to the invention of writing. For commerce, the invention removed the need to rely on memory. 'In these early times one must seek the germ of book-keeping'. Wagner suggests that the need to remember, and hence the utility of writing, could have occurred even with barter when the goods to be exchanged were not transferred simultaneously.

Commerce developed a new impetus with the introduction of money. Men, in whom avarice is inborn, greedily grasped this means to enrich themselves, and barter gave way to real selling and buying, and the scope of trading was enlarged. The need for recording and accounting was intensified, and, unless his affairs were to fall into confusion and decline, the merchant required to record his dealings in a certain order and to have some method of book-keeping. To be sure the account-books of the first merchants were vastly different from those of today, both as regards their material and form and also their contents.

In any case, early commerce lacked two essential things, which only later were to contribute greatly to its perfection: bills of exchange and postal services. Without these, trade was limited in extent and conducted at a slower pace. Nevertheless, the beginnings of book-keeping can be assigned to this early period, although the absence of records makes it fruitless to try to describe early book-keeping. This lack of information persists into the Middle Ages, until the ninth and tenth centuries. Then the Italian republics, notably the mighty Venice and Genoa, began to draw the entire trade of Europe to themselves. 'Naturally the large scale of business caused merchants to concern themselves increasingly with the question how to keep their books and records in a reliable, well-organised system'. Since most of the mercantile terms, both those used in merchandise trade and bills transactions and also those used in book-keeping itself are Italian, one can safely ascribe the invention of double-entry book-keeping to the Italians, and especially to the Venetians and Genoese. Indeed, the very name of the system is 'Italian double book-keeping'.

(Wagner welcomes the tendency observed by him for merchants increasingly to substitute German for foreign terms.)

The terms 'debit', 'credit' and 'account', and many others, were used in Venice and Genoa as early as the thirteenth century. Knowledge of the art passed to their northern neighbours in Germany, notably Augsburg and Nürnberg. 'The art flourished especially in Augsburg, where any man who understood the so-called Scrittura doppia was much esteemed and sought after'. The celebrated Fugger family firm of Augsburg employed skilled book-keepers. 'I myself have seen in a private library in Augsburg, a ledger of Antonius Fugger, kept between 1413 and 1427'. Wagner implies that it was kept on a double-entry basis.[20]

Wagner then turns to the literature of the subject. He owns a copy of one of the earliest works, Fra Paciolo's La Scuola perfetta dei mercanti etc, published in Venice in 1504, and which he describes in cryptic detail.[21] Various other works are mentioned. He observes also that in the late seventeenth century 'even various mathematicians busied themselves with the subject of book-keeping, and attempted to express it in algebraic formulae, as can be seen in the writings of Clairecombe, Ozanaman, Taquet etc.'.

His observations on seventeenth and eighteenth century publications are generally of little interest in the present context. He does, however, observe that some authors rejected double entry as being too prolix and unreliable, and presented simpler and shorter methods. Among these experts was Johann Christian Ferber of Husum, who in his book of 1712 gives a short description of a simple system of book-keeping, which he does not elaborate, however, because 'it is not double entry and rarely practised'. Wagner asks his reader ('every impartial and qualified person') whether this method is not the same as the English system of Jones. 'It is a pity', he says, 'that Ferber did not expound this system more fully, because if he had, he would have enriched the inventions made by Germans with an addition which now is claimed by a foreigner'. After further consideration of other works Wagner eventually concludes his historical survey by turning to Jones himself. 'And even if one cannot regard him as the real inventor [of his system], the honour nevertheless should be

[20]In Isler this ledger is dated 1419, a date repeated in Foster (1852). On the accounting of the Fugger, see Penndorf (1913), pp. 46 et seq; and Yamey (1975), p. 721, reprinted in Yamey (1978).

[21]On Wagner and the Scuola Perfetta, see Yamey (1974), reprinted in Yamey (1978).

accorded to him of having been the first to develop this method of book-keeping into a proper order'. Wagner, indeed, translated Jones's work of 1796, with his own modifications; but later he denounced the English system and criticised it severely.

F. W. Cronhelm makes some interesting comments in the 'Sketch of the Progress of Book-keeping' in his *Double Entry by Single* (1818).

Much of this sketch concerns the recording of possessions and debts without the benefit of writing or numbers. The sketch begins:

> The necessity of some record of property, and of the transactions affecting it, must have been felt in the earliest ages of society. The nature of the first rude expedients for this purpose, may be inferred from the allusions of ancient authors, from the customs of yet uncivilized tribes, and from the practice of ignorant and uninstructed persons within the circle of our own observation.

First he refers to occasional narrations by explorers of Africa and of the Pacific Islands of the use by primitive peoples of 'collections of pebbles, of shells, or of small pieces of wood' of different sizes and colours to designate 'single possessions and debts'. In these 'rude devices' 'we may discern not merely the dawn of Accounts, but the first germ of that symbolizing principle which has generated the noblest inventions, and the most fatal errors of mankind'.

Another 'contrivance consisted of notches cut on rods or canes'. He refers to the 'kindred expedient of knotted strings' of the Peruvians[22] as well as to the tallies introduced in England by Norman statesmen.

'The practice of scoring presents us with a third class of expedients for registering Accounts'. He observes that the custom of scores was in his day on the decline, 'but it may yet be traced on the chimney-board of the ale-house, and the wainscot of the village shop'.

He notes that the 'idea of durability seems to have been excluded from all these primitive attempts at accounts. When the balance was paid, the record was no longer preserved'.

From the primitives Cronhelm goes on to the Athenians. He believes that they did not keep permanent accounts even 'at the period of their highest refinement'. He cites also the parable of the faithless steward in the gospel of St. Luke to draw 'a similar inference of the want of durable accounts': '...had there been any permanent record of the debt, or, in other words, had any books been kept, the fraud would have been unavailing...'.

The Romans, by about the beginning of the Christian era, had, however, 'attained a permanent Method of Accounts, corresponding in all probability, to that of Single Entry'. And he refers to some of the Roman terminology first discussed by Stevin to whose 'researches' he expresses indebtedness. But the view of the 'ingenious Simon Stevin' that the Romans derived their book-keeping from the Greeks 'is very disputable, and far from being supported by the practice at Athens in the age of Demosthenes'. Although the Romans were not 'originally of a commercial character', commerce was extended when the Romans 'held united in peace as well as conquest, all the shores of the Mediterranean'. Thus he thinks it 'not improbable that Rome herself deserves the honour of inventing the method of Single Entry'. However, if an 'external origin must yet be sought, it may be no very presumptuous suggestion to indicate Carthage'. That unfortunate republic 'exceeded in commerce all the nations of antiquity; and, from her Asiatic origin and connexions, she possessed, in all probability, a system of numerals far more perfect than that of Rome'. The 'inglorious destruction of the Carthaginian records has placed...beyond determination' the conjecture that the Carthaginians invented single entry and 'may have communicated the art to her rival and destroyer'.

Skipping the centuries, Cronhelm turns to the fifteenth century and the revival of commerce and literature:

> Venice was in those days the great emporium of oriental and western commerce; and the adoption of the denary numbers by her merchants, was soon followed by the admirable, though complicated system of Accounts, named the Italian Method from the country of its invention, and Double Entry from the arrangement of its Ledger. Had it received a scientific denomination, it would have been called, from its balancing principle, the System of Equilibrium; or, with greater justice, it ought to have recorded the name of its inventor, now forgotten and unknown.

Then follows two short paragraphs on some authors of books on book-keeping, and a short,

---

[22]Coutereels (1623) refers to the *quipu* of Peru, according to Stevelinck (1970).

sharp criticism of Jones whose English system was 'intended to overthrow the Italian', but was 'abortive'. The final paragraph reads:

> Is it too much to hope, that England may yet enjoy the honour of perfecting the science of Accounts; and that, as she eclipses all that was wealth and glory in the commercial empires of the Mediterranean, so she may repay the debt of instruction, and restore to Italy the *Doppia Scrittura*, purified from its repetitions, and guarded from its liabilities to abuse?

Cronhelm may well have thought that his own modified system of double entry would serve this purpose.

In an important Dutch treatise of 1833, W. Oudshoff, described as 'book-keeper in Rotterdam', there is a short section 'On the Invention of Italian Book-keeping'. This consists almost entirely of a long quotation, translated from a foreign publication which he does not name and I cannot identify.

The first two paragraphs of the quoted material are clearly derived largely from Wagner: on barter and the importance of the introduction of writing and of money. But then follows a longer discussion of book-keeping in antiquity, the main burden of which is that the Romans were enemies of commerce and that the proud Roman held it to be beneath his dignity to be a merchant.

> We can therefore not look to the Romans for advances in scientific knowledge concerning trade; only after they had degenerated into weaklings because of their excessive luxury, and had as victims of their own weakness succumbed to the swords of the Barbarians, did their successors, the present-day Italians, begin to usher in a glorious period of commerce. Out of the ruins of Aquileia and other cities devastated by the Barbarians in their wrath, arose Venice, which later was to flourish.... To this fortunate period, when Mercury and the Muses chose the Hesperides for their realm, one must date the invention of an effective book-keeping system. At that time the commerce of Italy reached its highest level... Paper was invented; knowledge of discoveries was rapidly diffused by the art of printing...

The extract then refers to Pacioli's *Scuola perfetta* of 1504, evidently directly or indirectly derived from Wagner; but additionally it says that,

because of this early publication, some hold Pacioli to be the inventor of the Italian system, 'but probably it had been used earlier'.

Oudshoff comments, in conclusion, that he had not been able to discover more about the origins of double entry; 'but incomplete and uncertain as it may be, it is enough to show that the designation of the book-keeping system as "Italian" has no other purpose than to disclose the place or country where this art was invented'.

Foster and Carter

In 1852 the first book exclusively on the history of book-keeping was published in London: Benjamin Franklin Foster's *Origin and Progress of Book-keeping....* This book of 42 pages begins with a short essay. Of this, the first part is a long (acknowledged) extract from Cronhelm. Then come a few paragraphs on Pacioli and the 'first treatise' on book-keeping, taken (with acknowledgement) from the *Encyclopaedia Metropolitana*. Following this there is material taken, without direct or indirect acknowledgement, from Beckmann and Anderson, and a footnote from Wagner or one of his plagiarists (about Anthony Fugger's ledger, here dated 1419). After this disappointing essay Foster gives brief notices 'of the more celebrated works upon the subject of book-keeping which have appeared since the sixteenth century'. With one exception (Isler) the works dealt with are in English; the 'commentary' consists largely of extracts which, as the author says, 'have been greatly condensed, and without regard to the author's peculiar language or mode of expression'. Finally there is a list (with further extracts in some cases) of 159 'works on Book-keeping in the English language since 1543, of which One hundred and fifty-six are in the author's possession'.

F. Hayne Carter (1861; 2nd ed., 1874) has been quoted at the beginning of this article. His own remarks on the history of book-keeping cover three pages of the introduction to his book. These refer to various books on book-keeping, ranging in date from 1543 (Oldcastle) to 1828 (Tinwell). Almost all the books mentioned are in English. Some of his remarks would have puzzled his readers. Oldcastle (1543) is credited with a book called 'Treatise on the English Language'; John Collins, 'an eminent accountant and mathematician', is said on one page to have written a book 'which long served as a standard book on the subject', while on the next page the same book is one amongst those which 'were but little thought of'; and all we are told about 'the most concise and perfect volume of the kind' was that W. & R. Chambers of Edinburgh published it, and neither the author nor the date is named.[23]

Carter's rapid, selective and uninformative review of the earlier literature concludes with the following 'Advertisement' for his work:

> Having thus given the reader an opportunity of studying every variety of system, in many European tongues, modern as well as ancient, the author begs humbly to submit the following work, explanatory of Book-keeping by Double and Single Entry, in the earnest hope that a Science hitherto considered difficult of attainment, may be better understood and more highly appreciated, when its real simplicity is made apparent.

A concluding note

As we have seen, several of the early authors were interested in attempts to locate the place and time of the birth of the double-entry system which most of them expounded in their own books. But there is remarkably little in their commentaries on the development within that system of such features as the use of subsidiary account-books, or the procedures for closing the ledger, or the accounting treatment of durable assets. Almost no curiosity is expressed about the evolution of double-entry book-keeping technique. Indeed, the commentaries surveyed here generally seem to treat the introduction of double entry as the last significant historical event.

Certainly, statements can be found to the effect that there could be no improvement on that system, and that any changes in book-keeping practice were no more than minor modifications made within its structure. Oudshoff (1833) expressed himself in these terms: 'Changes may be made—as would be a natural consequence of the influence of advancing civilisation—in the outward form, such as has already happened from time to time, as can easily be shown; but the foundations on which the science is based remain incapable of improvement'. (Oudshoff did not exemplify the changes which had already taken place.) It is of interest that our author made the quoted statement after he had drawn attention to the various attempts which had been made (starting with Jones) to supplant double entry by a different system capable of achieving the same objective

more simply and with less trouble. Oudshoff reports that these attempts had failed; and he asserts that similar attempts were doomed to failure, because the double-entry system was securely founded on scientific principles.

Successful revolution was considered impossible, not only by Oudshoff. And, in comparison with the momentous invention of double entry, subsequent evolutionary modifications and adaptations may have seemed too peripheral to deserve the attention of chroniclers or speculative historians.

References

Ames, J., *Typographical antiquities...*, London, 1749.
Anderson, A., *An historical and chronological deduction of the origin of commerce...*, London, 1764.
Barrême, B. F., *Traité des parties doubles...*, Paris, 1721.
Beckmann, J., *Beyträge zur Geschichte der Erfindungen*, Leipzig, 1783.
Idem., *Anweisung die Rechnungen kleiner Haushaltungen zu führen*, Göttingen, 1797.
Idem., *History of inventions and discoveries*, translated by W. Johnston, London 1814 (2nd ed).
Boucher, P., *La Science des négocians...*, Paris, 1803.
Buse, G. H., *Allgemeiner kaufmännischer Buchhalter...*, Erfurt, 1804.
Carter, F. H., *Practical book-keeping...*, Edinburgh, 1861.
Cronhelm, F. W., *Double entry by single*, London, 1818.
Coutereels, J., *L'Art solide de livre de comptes...*, Middelburg, 1623.
Dafforne, R., *The merchants mirrour...*, London, 1635.
Ferber, J. C., *Wohlunterrichteten Kaufmann*, Hamburg, 1712.
Foster, B. F., *The origin and progress of book-keeping...*, London, 1852.
Flori, L., *Trattato del modo di tenere il libro doppio domestico...*, Palermo, 1636.
Gammersfelder, S., *Buchhalten durch zwey bücher...*, Danzig, 1570.
(van) Gezel, W., *Kort begrijp van 't beschouwig onderwijs in 't koopmans boekhouden...*, Amsterdam, 1681.
Gordon, W., *The universal accountant...*, Edinburgh, 1754 (2nd ed).
Gottlieb, J., *Ein teutsch verstendig Buchhalten...*, Nürnberg, 1531.
Grimm, K. F., *Anleitung zur doppelten italienischen Buchhaltung*, Cassel, 1828.
Hager, C. A., *Buchhalten...*, Hamburg, 1660.
Hamilton, A. book review, *Monthly Review*, vol 26, 1798 (p. 129).
Inglis, W., *Book-keeping by single and double entry...*, Edinburgh and London, 1849.
Irson, J., *Méthode pour bien dresser toutes sortes de comptes...*, Paris, 1687.
Isler, J., *Nouvelle méthode suisse, pour tenir les livres...*, Brussels, 1810.
Jones, E. T., *English system of book-keeping...*, Bristol, 1796.
Kelly, P., *The Elements of book-keeping...*, London, 1801.
Kock, D., *De luchtende fackel van het italiaens boeckhouden*, Amsterdam, 1658 (B. H. Geestevelt, ed.)
Leuchs, J. M., *Theorie und Praxis des Italienischen Buchhaltens...*, Nürnberg, 1806.
Littleton, A. C., and B. S. Yamey (eds), *Studies in the history of accounting*, London, 1956 (reprinted New York, 1978).
Macpherson, D., *Annals of commerce...*, London, 1805.
Manzoni, D., *Quaderno doppio...*, Venice 1540.

---

[23]Carter may have had in mind Inglis (1849), a publication which went into several editions.

Mellema, E. E. L., *Boeckhouder na de conste van Italien...*, Franicker, 1590.

Moschetti, G. A., *Dell' universal trattato di libri doppii...*, Venice, 1610.

North, R., *The Gentleman Accomptant*, London, 1714.

Oldcastle, H., *A profitable treatyce...*, London, 1543.

Oudshoff, W., *Volledig theoretisch en praktisch handboek voor het Italiaansch of koopmans boekhouden*, Rotterdam, 1833.

Pacioli, L., *Summa di arithmetica...*, Venice, 1494.

Peele, J., *The pathe waye to perfectnes...*, London, 1569.

Penndorf, B., *Geschichte der Buchhaltung in Deutschland*, Leipzig, 1913.

Pietersz, N., *Practicque om te leeren rekenen cypheren ende boeckhouwen...*, Amsterdam, 1583.

(de la) Porte, M., *La Science des Negocians...*, new ed., Paris, 1753.

Rees, A., *The cyclopaedia; or, universal dictionary of arts, sciences, and literature*, vol. 5, London 1819.

(de) Renterghem, B., *Instruction nouvelle pour tenir le livre de compte...*, Antwerp, 1592.

Schreiber, H., *Ayn new kunstlich Buech...*, Nürnberg, 1518.

Schweicker, W., *Zwifach Buchhalten*, Nürnberg, 1549.

Stevelinck, E., catalogue entries, *La comptabilité à travers les âges*, Brussels, 1970.

Stevin, S., *Vorstelicke bouckhouding op de Italiaensche wyse...*, Leiden, 1607.

(de) Waal, P. G. A., *De leer van het boekhouden in der Nederlanden tijdens de 16e eeuw*, Roermond, 1927.

Wagner, A., *Eduard T. Jones neuerfundene einfache und doppelte Englische Buchhalterey...*, Leipzig, 1801.

Weddington, J., *A breffe instruction and manner howe to kepe merchants bokes of accomptes...*, Antwerp, 1567.

Woolf, A. H., *A short history of accountants and accountancy...*, London, 1913.

Yamey, B. S., 'Fifteenth and sixteenth century manuscripts on the art of book-keeping', *Journal of Accounting Research*, vol. 5, 1967.

Idem., 'Luca Pacioli's 'Scuola Perfetta': a bibliographical puzzle', *Gutenberg-Jahrbuch*, 1974.

Idem., 'Notes on double-entry book-keeping and economic progress' *Journal of European Economic History*, vol. 4, 1975.

Idem., *Essays on the history of accounting*, New York, 1978.

Ympyn, J., *Nieuwe instructie...*, Antwerp, 1543.

JAMES PEELE IN CONTEXT

PEELE'S TWO TREATISES IN CONTEXT

B. S. Yamey

1. PUBLICATIONS ON BOOKKEEPING AND ACCOUNTING, 1494–1569

The earliest printed exposition of double-entry bookkeeping is the section (" distinctio ") on the subject in Luca Pacioli's compendious *Summa* published in Venice in 1494.[1] Several works in the Paciolian mould were published in the first half of the sixteenth century: in Italian, Manzoni (1540); in Dutch (Flemish), Ympyn (1543), a work which also appeared in a French version (1543) and in an English version (1547); in English, also Oldcastle (1543); and in German (*via* Manzoni), Schweicker (1549).[2] Although these works resemble Pacioli's closely in many respects, they nevertheless exhibit several, sometimes major, "deviations" from the pioneering text by way of modifications, omissions and additions.

The earliest works in German were independent of the Paciolian tradition, although they too dealt with the double-entry system. Schreiber (1518) has a short part on bookkeeping, in which the system is illustrated in a set of account-books. Two distinguishing features are, first, the separation of the ledger into two books, the book of debts and the book of merchandise; and second, the profit calculation which is not so neatly integrated into the rest of the bookkeeping as it is in the Venetian system. Schreiber's book appeared in several editions, under somewhat different titles. In the period covered here it was also plagiarised in Kaltenbrunner (1565) and Hübner (1567).

The first Italian author after Pacioli's pioneering work was Tagliente, a prolific writer on a wide range of subjects from calligraphy to the composition of love-letters.

---

(1) Books referred to by author's name and date are listed, with more details, in the References on pp. 71-2.

(2) I do not pursue here the question whether the Paciolian treatises are derived directly from Pacioli (1494) or whether, instead, they (or some of them) as well as Pacioli have their origin in some unknown Venetian manuscript. On this question, see Yamey (1967) for a review of rival contentions and of the evidence.

To the developing literature on bookkeeping he contributed two slim books, both published in 1525, which deal respectively with double entry and single entry (the former also published in another edition, 1533). In 1525, an anonymous and insignificant booklet on bookkeeping was published, also in Venice. This slight work was the forerunner of several other anonymous pamphlets or booklets which were published in Venice and are of no interest for the history of the development of the subject.[3] The Venetian, Alvise Casanova (1558), referred to one of these opuscules as well as to one of Tagliente's works as being fit only to be used as wrapping-paper for pilchards.[4]

Gottlieb was the second German writer on bookkeeping. His first book, of 1531, devoted wholly to bookkeeping, resembles Schreiber's in the two-fold division of the ledger, although Gottlieb prefers that the two divisions should be in a single book. His work was followed by von Ellenbogen in 1537, who criticised his model for not having shown how a set of accounts are to be balanced and closed. Von Ellenbogen made good the deficiency, in a manner reminiscent of Schreiber (1518). And in 1546 Gottlieb in a second work also illustrated the closing procedure and profit calculation which he had omitted in his earlier work.

In 1539, the year before the publication in Venice of Manzoni's Paciolian treatise, Cardano's *Practica arithmetice* was published in Milan, in Latin. The sixtieth chapter ("De ratione librorum tractandorum") is about bookkeeping. Such interest as it has derives from the fame of its author, a prominent philosopher, mathematician and physician.

Manzoni (1540, and later editions), Ympyn (1543; 1547) and Oldcastle (1543) have already been noted, as has Schweicker (1549)—six publications in one decade, all distinctly in the Paciolian tradition. The only other work in this decade still to be introduced is de Texada's *Suma de Arithmetica* (1545 and 1546). This book, in Spanish, concludes with a short discussion of a simple (not double-entry) system of accounts designed for a nobleman with an extensive estate.

The major works on bookkeeping by Mennher, a German who settled in Antwerp, were published in that city between 1550 and 1565. His first book, in French,

---

(3) One of these booklets is not anonymous, but is written by Bartolomeo Fontana.

(4) "...queste due ho veduto, vi dico che sono carte da sardelle". These words occur in a prefatorial dialogue between Casanova and a friend. They are spoken by the friend after Casanova had referred to a work "che insegna a tener libro ordinariamente." sold by a blind pedlar on the Rialto bridge in Venice. Casanova (1558). The judgment on Tagliente is undeservedly harsh.

illustrates a simple system of accounts to be kept by an agent or factor for his principal. In this system there is a ledger for personal accounts and a separate book for merchandise accounts.

It is at this point in the chronology that James Peele's first book (1553) makes its appearance, that is, shortly after the publication of the six Paciolian treatises of the 1540's, two of which were in English.

Between Peele's first book and his second book (1569) the principal works published were by Mennher, Casanova (1558), Savonne (1567) and, most important, Weddington (1567), the latter the only publication in English during the period.

2. METHODS OF EXPOSITION

Pacioli (1494) explains in chapter 33 that each transaction must be entered twice in the ledger, once in debit and once in credit (" ...tutte le partite che se metteno al libro hano a essere doppie: cioe se tu fai uno creditore al si fare uno debitore "). Several later authors were to emphasise that the skill of the accountant lay in the ability to distinguish, for any transaction, the two ledger accounts to be debited and credited respectively. Manzoni (1540) writes (in the eleventh chapter on the journal) that the difficulty of the art was in knowing how to discern in each transaction what is to be the debtor, what the creditor (" ...consiste tutta la difficulta de l'arte, in saper discernere in ciascuna facenda, qual sia esse debitore, e creditore "). Effective instruction required that the reader or student should acquire this knowledge and so be able to disentangle and record the dual aspects of every transaction in both the journal and the ledger.

Pacioli's pioneering treatise does not score high marks on this test. No general rules or guiding principles are set out. And there is no comprehensive illustrative set of accounts to serve as a model. At best, scattered in the main body of the text are isolated examples illustrating the treatment of particular transactions. Indeed, from the point of view of the reader, in the present context the most useful part of the entire section is to be found at a place where it could easily have been overlooked. Following on after the last numbered chapter, which is entitled " summary ", there is an unnumbered part headed " Matters to be placed in the book of merchants " (" Casi che apartiene a mettere al libro de' mercanti ").

This part consists of five paragraphs. It tells the reader how to proceed in respect of each of several types of transaction. Here is the first passage of the exposition concerning purchases:

> If you should buy merchandise or other things for cash, make that particular
> merchandise or thing debtor, and cash creditor. If you should say, " I did not
> buy the merchandise for cash, as above, but a bank will pay for me, or indeed
> one of my friends will pay for me", then I will reply to you that in any case
> you must make the particular merchandise debtor, as said above: but where I
> told you to make cash creditor, you should make creditor that bank or that
> friend of yours who has paid for you.[5]

The exposition then elaborates further possibilities; notes that for sales one proceeds
as for purchases, except that one puts things in the opposite way (" ...salvo ch'ai
a mettere per lo opposito "); and goes on to explain what is meant.

This method of listing the treatment of different types of transaction, usually
grouped according to their general character (e. g. purchases), is to be found in
several of the treatises in the period up to 1569. The effectiveness of this form
of instruction was, of course, much enhanced by the provision of illustrative sets
of transactions entered into the specimen account-books. Thus the short expository
text in Schreiber (1518) consists largely of ten " rules " which tell the reader what
to do for each of various types of transaction.

An improvement was to link, by cross-references, each particular proposition or
rule in the expository text with the corresponding illustrative entry (or entries) in
the specimen account-books. This is the method used by Peele in both his books. It
is facilitated by the consecutive numbering of the journal entries — a practice which
at the time was used by some merchants and which first finds its way into the literature in Manzoni (1540). Manzoni, however, unlike Peele, does not include in his
text a complete set of propositions or particular rules governing each of the types of

---

(5) " Compre che tu facessi di mercantie o di che cosa si fusse per li denari contanti debbi
fare debitore quelle tale mercantia o quella tale cosa e creditore la cassa. E se tu dicessi.
Io [non] la comprai a denari contanti comme e ditto. Ma una banco gli pago per me, o
veramente uno mio amico gli pago per me. Rispondoti che a ogni modo hai a fare debitore
quella tale mercantia comme di sopra o ditto. Ma dove io ti dissi farai creditore la cassa
tu hai a fare creditore quel banco, o quello tuo amico che per te gli a pagati."
  The word " non " in square brackets is not in the original, but is obviously required for
sense, as is indicated in Antinori's transcription (1959).
  It may be noted that the " Casi " section in Pacioli, from which the passage is taken, has
no counterpart in Ympyn (1543) or Oldcastle (1543). Its inclusion may be seen as a piece
of evidence supporting the conjecture that all three authors used an earlier manuscript, and
that Pacioli made some *ad hoc* additions to his version of it.

transaction illustrated in the model set of accounts. He gives some detailed guidance on the treatment of the acquisition and disposal of goods (in chapter 11 on the journal). But most of the types of transaction illustrated in the 300 journal entries in the model set of accounts are merely listed, suitably grouped by their nature, in a comprehensive table (" tavola ") indicating the type of the transaction (but not its treatment as to debit and credit), in each case with references to the numbered journal entry which exemplifies it and the folios of the two ledger accounts affected. Thus one group of entries in the table is " of the purchase of merchandise, and other things, in various ways " (" Di comprar mercantie, & altre cose, in diversi modi "); it has eleven entries, the first of which is for cash purchases.

In addition, in the model journal Manzoni indicates the type of transaction at the side of each entry. This device was followed, with modification, by Peele in his first book, but was discarded for the second.

The basic expository method described above —as well as variants of it[6]— enabled the reader or user to find out, quite easily and conveniently, how he was to treat, as to debit and credit, any particular transaction of a type covered in the exposition. But it did not tell him how to treat a type of transaction which was not covered in the enumeration or illustration. Further, since it did not explain the logical derivation of the stated rules for particular transactions, the user either had to refer to the treatise whenever in difficulty or else he had to memorise the rules parrot-wise.

The first attempt at the formulation of general guidelines or principles —as distinct from detailed rules, each specific to a particular type of transaction— is in Gottlieb (1531). Gottlieb explains that it is natural that what is owing to a creditor should be on the right-hand (credit) side of the ledger because the right hand signifies good faith (" ...dieweyl traw unnd glaub durch die rechte handt bedeut wirdt "). Again, goods received should naturally be entered on the first or left-hand (debit) side of the ledger and goods sold on the credit side, because buying or possessing must precede selling (" ...dieweyl ye dz kauffen oder haben vor dem verkauffen geet "). It is doubtful whether these contrived explanations would have

---

(6) Variants of the procedure in which a class of transaction is described and then illustrated in an illustrative journal entry are to be found in Tagliente (1525), Gottlieb (1531 ; 1546) and Mennher (1565).

Tagliente is interesting for several entries dealing with the receipt of a dowry and its disposal after the death of the wife. An account " rason de dotta " is involved. Such occurrences, also found in Manzoni, are not dealt with in either of Peele's treatises.

helped any bookkeeper in his tasks—and, likewise, the prescription above the ledger in von Ellenbogen (1537) to this effect : If I pay, put it on debit side ; if I am paid, on the credit (" Zalet ich, setz auf sol mir, Zalet mir auff sol ich [7] ").

In the eleventh chapter on the journal in Manzoni (1540), which itself owes little or nothing to Pacioli, the author seems on the point of enunciating some general principle to cover the treatment of selling, buying, receiving, paying, bartering, lending, donating, " and many other things " (" ...& i moltissime altre cose "). He refers to four components (" quatro termini ") which the merchant should always have in mind, because they apply to all his transactions. These four " termini " are : one who gives, the other who receives, and the thing given or received, and also the cause (" ...cioe uno che da, l'altro che riceve, et quella cosa che vien data o ricevuta, & anche la causa... "). However, this formulation is then applied solely to five different ways in which goods may pass into or out of a business : for cash, on credit, against a bank payment, against a promise from or to another, or in barter. Each of these ways is then dealt with in turn. But the more general application or applicability of the formulation is not explained or demonstrated. And in the following chapter, a firm rule (" regola ferma ") is limited to buying and selling transactions.

In the *Maner and fourme* Peele enunciates a general rule. At the end of the fourth chapter, in which the treatment of numerous types of occurrence is detailed, he refers to a " generall rule " which should be marked well. This rule is : " to make the thinge or thinges received, debitour to the thynge or thynges delivered, or the receyver debitour to the deliverer ". With this rule, and the other instructions, " you cannot mysse ". In the next chapter the notion is elaborated and the rule changed slightly :

> You shall understande, that every one parcell in the Jornall, ought to bee twoo in the Quaterne, and the cause is, that every of theim dooeth include or contain twoo properties, wherof thone is a debitour, or borower, and the other is a Creditour or lender. The borower, or the thyng borowed, is become Debitour, by reason that it dooeth retain and possesse : and the lender, or the thyng lent, is the Creditour, by reason that it is dispossessed.

In the opening part of this passage, it may be noted, there is some echo of Ympyn (1547):

---

(7) See Penndorf (1913), p. 119.

Ye must understand that every parcell whiche must be entred into the boke [journal] contaigneth in itself two contraries in nature the one to the other. That is to saie a debitor, whiche is he that oweth, and the creditor, that is he that lendeth or that it is owyng unto.

In the versified "Rules to be observed" which precede the ledger in Peele's specimen set of account-books the rule becomes:

> To make the thinges Receivyd, or the receiver,
> Debter to the thinges delivered, or to the deliverer.

Peele does not demonstrate how this rule is to be put to use in respect of any awkward transaction or occurrence. In his *Pathe waye* of 1569, Peele repeats the rule in the form: "All thinges receaved, or the receaver, must owe to all thinges delivered, or to the deliverer". This rule, the schoolmaster tells his scholar, is to be learned "by rote, and also by reason"; and if it is "well understanded", it will help him to master the art of making proper entries in the journal.[8] The scholar answers that he has already mastered the rule by rote, but "the reason thereof I understande not". The schoolmaster's explication is in "fewe wordes", and is in terms of the application of the rule in simple cases involving buying and selling and receiving and paying cash.

One of the well-known weaknesses of the general rule is encountered later in the treatise, when the first journal entry to involve the profit-and-loss account is being discussed. The latter account is to be debited for an amount credited to a debtor's account as rebate for early settlement of a bill. The master explains that the profit-and-loss account contains losses on the debit side and gains on the credit side. The scholar, who has said that the rebate should be debited to the account because there is a loss on the settlement of the bill, is asked whether he can "perceave the common rule to be observed herein". To which he replies: "...and because losse is susteyned (whiche after a certayne maner is received) thaccompte of losse and gayne is made debter...".

In spite of the evident deficiencies of Peele's rule, didactic formulations such as his, often with some extensions, persisted into the nineteenth (and possibly even

---

(8) Peele says the rule "is to be practised in all causes of entring percelles into the Journall for the moste parte..."; the last four words suggest that the limitations of the rule were recognised by Peele.

twentieth) century. One finds such a formulation in the work of the influential and intelligent Dutchman, Oudshoff, in the first half of the nineteenth century. In his *Volledig handboek* (1833) he discussed this "general main rule" ("algemeenen hoofdregel") in terms of the personification of non-personal accounts; and he observes justly (if somewhat exaggeratedly) that with such a single general rule "which is applicable to each entry, irrespective of its nature, people have been satisfied for three centuries because they have regarded it, correctly, as wholly adequate"[9].

A novel feature of Peele's *Pathe waye* is that the text is cast in the form of two dialogues[10], the first between the schoolmaster and a merchant who comes to him with an accounting problem, and the second between the schoolmaster and the scholar. The dialogue form was to become popular with writers on bookkeeping, and its use is often tedious and irritating. Peele's use of the artificial device is, in the main, rather attractive and even charming. Thus the first dialogue, in which the schoolmaster shows up the shortcomings of the merchant's confused and limited accounting system, ends with the satisfied merchant asking the teacher to "accepte this small rewarde", and promising to send his "man" to him for proper instruction. The second dialogue has many nice touches, as the reader will observe: they possibly helped to lighten the task of a pupil trying to master the mysteries of double entry.

3. BALANCING, CLOSING AND RE-OPENING THE LEDGER

In his first book of 1531 Gottlieb deliberately omitted any exposition or illustration of the closing of the account-books and their re-opening. He claimed that it was

---

(9) Oudshoff (1833), p. 303. He states the rule in this form:

Al wie ontvangt
Al wat ontvangt } is Debet

Al wie uitgeeft
Al wat uitgeeft } is Credit

An earlier example of the general rule for debits is in Hayes (1741):
   The Grand General Rule.
   All Things received, or the Receiver,
                    or,
   The Account upon which the Thing is received,
         must always be made Debtor.
   There is a corresponding rule for credits.

(10) Reference has already been made (in footnote 4) to the dialogue in Casanova (1558); but that dialogue is in the preface to the book, "Ragionamento d'Alvise Casanova et un suo amico".

very difficult to explain these processes in writing and that the student would not in any case derive much help from written expositions. In this matter an hour of practical demonstration and face-to-face teaching was far more productive. He therefore decided to spare his readers; and he advised them that, if they wished to learn how to effect the closing of the books and to acquire other obscure skills ("verporgner geschickligkeyt"), they should come to him for oral instruction.

Gottlieb exaggerated the difficulties. But it is nevertheless highly likely that the contemporary reader of Pacioli's treatment of the closing of the ledger would have been confused and puzzled. Although some parts of the exposition are excellent, notably that relating to the checking of the ledger entries against the journal entries, other parts are unsatisfactory. Two methods for closing a ledger are confused; and the discussion of the "summa summarum" (a form of trial balance) is so cryptic that it led Manzoni (1540) into error and still poses a conundrum for modern commentators.[11]

Pacioli's task as expositor was aggravated by his decision not to provide an illustrative set of account-books. The inclusion of comprehensive worked examples made it possible for those who came after him to content themselves with much shorter expositions in their texts. Thus Ympyn (1543) treats the closing procedures briefly in his text: but the short exposition is admirably complemented by the example in the model account-books. Ympyn's book is the first in the literature to include a balance account as an account (the last account) in the balanced and closed ledger,[12] and it is also the first in which the opening entries in the new ledger are also illustrated, so that the reader would have had no difficulty in practice in raising a new ledger out of the remains of its predecessor.

In each of his two books Peele also shows the opening of the new ledger with its initial entries (although in the *Maner and fourme* the clarity of the demonstration is reduced by the inclusion of entries for some partnership transactions — which

---

(11) On Pacioli's treatment of the balancing and closing of the ledger, see Yamey (1977).

(12) Gottlieb (1546) includes a kind of closing balance account, in the description of which the author uses the metaphor of a balance or scale ("Wag"). The opening words on each side of the account are "To close this trading or account" ("Diesen Handel oder Rechnung zu beschliessen..."). Schweicker (1549) departs from its model [Manzoni (1540)] by including a closing balance account. The opening words on each side of the account suggest derivation from Gottlieb: "Zubeschliessen disz Buch oder dise rechnung...". As was shown in Kheil (1896), Schweicker's worked example has several errors. The equilibrium of the balance account is achieved only by means of a single entry on the debit side. This amount is then incongruously posted to the credit of the re-opened capital account.

seems to have been an afterthought).

However, in the *Maner and fourme* Peele did not follow Ympyn in other respects. In Peele's balance account ("ballaunce of accompt") in the old ledger the balances on the capital ("stocke") account and the profit-and-loss account are shown separately, whereas in Ympyn's example the closing balance on the latter account is transferred to the capital account, the closing balance of which appears in the balance account. Further, unlike in Ympyn, Peele has a sort of opening balance account in the new ledger. In this account —"Remain of balaunce in the last yeres accompte"— the individual asset account balances are shown on the credit side and the creditors' account balances on the debit. The counterbalancing entries for these entries in the "remain" account are shown appropriately in debit or credit in the new accounts in the new ledger. The "remain" account is balanced with an entry: "This reste taken on Creditour side, is the owners net substaunce, borne to Balaunce in folio...". But there is no folio reference, nor indeed any capital account in the opened new ledger. Had Peele at this stage made a post-inventory trial balance of the kind referred to early in the second dialogue in his treatise of 1569, he would have seen that in the new ledger it was not the case that "every debitour hathe his creditour, and everye creditour his debitour".

Peele's intentions are not clear. It is possible that he intended the balance account in the new ledger to be an *opening* balance account in which the entries in the preceding ledger's *closing* balance account are repeated but reversed. Had Peele shown the opening balance of the new capital account, his intention would not have been in doubt. And, as Kats noted,[13] had he done so, his reversed opening balance account would have been the first example in the literature of this procedure, which had already been used in some merchants' accounts.[14] Alternatively, and less likely, the account in question might have been intended to serve as the capital account in the new ledger. But the inclusion in it of the entry for the (non-executed) transfer of the balance goes against this interpretation.

Between 1553 and 1569 three books were published in which the erection of a reversed opening balance account is correctly incorporated in the balancing and closing process. The earliest instance is in Casanova (1558), although the author did not explain the rationale of the particular procedure.[15] Weddington (1567) de-

---

(13) Kats (1930), p. 42.
(14) For a more detailed discussion of this procedure, see Yamey (1970).

scribes, explains and illustrates the opening balance account. According to him, through it "you shall in Debitor and Creditor lincke, the one great Boke [ledger], withe the other". Savonne (1567) also describes the reversed opening balance account. He explains that it is necessary for technical bookkeeping reasons, and also because with this account at the beginning of a ledger there is no need to have recourse to its predecessor.[15]

Although Peele's second book was influenced by Weddington's, he did not introduce this particular innovation in it. Instead, the ledger-closing procedures owe much more to Ympyn.

In his *Maner and fourme* Peele shows awareness of Ympyn's example. In the eighth chapter he says that there are "other waies to make your Ballaunce, and all commeth to one effect"; but it would be profitless to speak of them in this book "for that one onely ordre can but be taught in one booke". He mentions two specific practices: first, "...to bryng your gooddes remainyng therunto, in one totall, bearyng the particulers into a new Quaterne booke [ledger], from eche several accompt"; and second, "havyng a double Folio in your Ballaunce". Both these practices are to be found in Ympyn and in no other work before 1553; and both appear also in the *Pathe waye*.

Ympyn transfers all the closing balances of the individual merchandise accounts into a single account, which is then transferred to the (closing) balance account. This collective account is re-opened in the new ledger, and then promptly closed by carrying the individual amounts to the various re-opened merchandise accounts. Peele does the same in the *Pathe waye*, with a difference to be noted shortly. Neither Ympyn nor Peele explains the purpose of the "goodes remayninge" account. Presumably it was part of a tidying-up operation to relieve the balance account of several entries; or possibly, but improbably, it was to obtain a useful sub-total to appear in the final balance account. It may be noted, in passing, that in Schweicker

---

(15) In the copy of Casanova (1558) examined by me, the placing of the account balances in the closing balance account is the same as that in the opening balance account, that is, assets on the credit side, and capital etc. on the debit side. The entries in the journal are correct, however. The error is not noted in the errata list, but the author or printer did add: "Molti altri errori sono incorsi, i quali per brevità si lassano".

It is interesting that Casanova shows the capital and profit-and-loss account balances separately in the balance account, as is also done in the closing balance account in Peele's *Maner and fourme*.

(16) See de Waal (1927), p. 151.

(1549) the debtors' and creditors' balances respectively are gathered together in two collective accounts, in preparation for the opening of the balance account.

In Peele's *Pathe waye* there are two posting reference columns on each side of the balance account in the first (" A ") ledger, headed " A " and " B " respectively.[17] It is explained that in the A column one inserts the folio number of the account in the A ledger whence the particular entry came; and in the B column one inserts the folio number of the account opened in the new (B) ledger. Ympyn used the same device. In this way the same closing balance account served also as the source for the opening entries in the new ledger, thereby avoiding the need for an opening balance account or opening journal entries in the new ledger. Peele writes that in this fashion " I have used as muche brevite as maye posible be put in practise, and have rejected the tediousnes that divers use therin ". He went further than Ympyn in this direction, however, in that he also furnished his " goodes remayninge " account with two posting columns and therefore had no need to raise an (opening) collective account in the new ledger. Peele was able to improve upon his model.

4. OTHER SELECTED FEATURES

(a) Simple and compound journal entries

In the fifth chapter of the *Maner and fourme* Peele stresses " that every one parcell [entry] in the Jornall, ought to bee twoo in the Quaterne [ledger]...", in these words echoing statements to be found in Pacioli and other early writers. These statements imply that each journal entry indicates one ledger account to be debited and another to be credited. Simple journal entries of this kind are the only ones to be found illustrated in Pacioli, Tagliente, Manzoni, Ympyn and Peele (1553).

However, examples of compound journal entries are to be found in the early practice of double entry[18] — that is, a journal entry in which more than one ledger account is to be debited (or credited), for example where goods are sold partly for cash and partly on credit. Pacioli was well aware of this practice. In his eleventh chapter he talks about " either one or several accounts to be debited or credited

---

(17) In Peele's *Pathe waye* the first ledger is marked with the letter A and the second with B. This usage is also in Casanova (1558) and Weddington (1567). In Peele's earlier *Maner and fourme* the first ledger is marked with the sign of the cross and the second with the letter A—as in Pacioli (1494), Manzoni (1540) and Ympyn (1543).

(18) For early Tuscan practice, see Melis (1962), pp. 421-4. For a Milanese example of 1457, see Zerbi (1952), p. 381.

from a journal entry" ("...el debitore o uno o piu..."). Manzoni (1540) does the same. And in the third chapter of the *Maner and fourme* Peele also recognises the possibility when he says that "one figure or figures" (referring to one or more ledger accounts) may have to be inserted in the ledger-posting reference column of the journal above (or below) the "litle overthwart stroke". Presumably compound journal entries were not illustrated in the treatises because any complex transaction can be decomposed into a set of simple journal entries, and because simple entries illustrate the dual nature of transactions more clearly (at least for beginners) than compound entries.

Examples of compound journal entries are encountered in the non-Paciolian works of Schreiber (1518), Gottlieb (1531 ; 1546), von Ellenbogen (1537) and Mennher (1550).[19] Gottlieb, however, does not show the full practical advantage of the use of compound entries. He enters each of the constituent parts of the joint debit (or credit) separately in the corresponding credit (or debit) in the relevant ledger account.

Weddington (1567) is the first English treatise to use compound journal entries; and they are to be found also in Peele's *Pathe waye*. Although the method for indicating in the journal the postings to the various ledger accounts is different in the two books, it is likely that Peele had been influenced by the treatise published two years earlier than his own. Peele introduces the use of compound entries in dealing with his 38th type of transaction. He takes the case where a debtor is allowed a rebate for paying his account before the agreed date. He first shows two examples in the journal in which the transaction is decomposed into two simple entries. He then illustrates two compound entries for the same type of transaction. (He also shows the two alternative treatments for some other types of transaction). He uses the term "Reperticion apertayning to sundrie accomptes" to stand for the several accounts to be debited (as against the single account to be credited); the constituent accounts are then itemised. Peele explains that compound journal entries economise on entries in the ledger : "...which order in some percelles [transactions] will do great ease, for happely a man maye bye or sell, at one instant many percelles [parcels *or* lots] of or to some one man, then by this order of repartinge : there needes but one somme in the margent of the Leager...".

I have not encountered the term "repartition" or "repetition" (which means division or distribution) in early practice, where such terms as "severals" or

(19) Mennher did not use this type of entry in his later book (1565).

94

" sundries " were used.   But Dafforne (1635) writes as though Peele's term was used by merchants.

(b) Quantity columns in goods accounts

In a popular eighteenth-century treatise John Mair (1736) writes :

> A Merchant may, at any time, know what Goods he has on hand, by comparing the inner Columns of the *Accompts of Goods*, without being put to the Trouble of inspecting his Ware-house, and weighing or measuring the Goods themselves.

Mair is referring here to the common practice of having separate ledger accounts for each distinct type of goods and of having columns for entries of quantities immediately to the left of the money columns—a practice which provided a kind of perpetual inventory control.   In the literature of bookkeeping and accounts the notion of a multiplicity of separate goods accounts goes back to Pacioli.   But quantity columns are first used in Mennher (1550).   Weddington (1567) was the first to illustrate them in an English treatise ; but in his book the columns are placed at the left-hand margin of the ledger page.[20]   Peele does not have quantity columns in the *Maner and fourme*.   They do appear in the *Pathe waye*, placed in the same position in the ledger accounts as in Weddington.   This seems to be an instance of a direct borrowing from Weddington.

Some of the early writers who did not have quantity columns in their ledgers nevertheless emphasised the need for control over quantities and included details of the quantities involved in the entries in the various goods accounts.   This emphasis is even more readily evident in Ympyn (1543), Gottlieb (1546) and Mennher's later work (1565) in which the quantities noted in entries on each side of a goods account are totalled and balanced.

(c) Secret accounts

The use of secret ledgers was well established in practice long before they were

---

[20] Quantity columns on the left-hand side of each ledger page are to be found in the ledger, 1538-1550, of the English merchant, John Smythe. See Vanes (1974). The quantity columns in this ledger were not always balanced. Several accounts, however, show careful attention to the balancing of the entries for quantities ; see for example, pp. 238-40, where the account of " seckes " (sack, a kind of white wine) has an entry :" 2 buttes owt, 2 buttes to yllage [ullage] & 3 buttes drounck & wast ". (The Smythe ledger was not kept on the double-entry system). Similarly-placed quantity columns are also to be found in several of the goods accounts in the surviving ledger (1522 to 1528) of Thomas Howell, in the archives of the Drapers' Company, London. (This ledger also was not kept in double entry).

discussed in the accounting literature. There is, however, in Pacioli's treatise some consideration of the concealment of accounting information from clerks or others who had access to some of the account-books but not to all. Pacioli says in his tenth chapter that the entries in the inventory book or records should be entered in the journal and that, because the journal is " your secret book" (" tuo libro secreto "), the merchant could record all his possessions, including his non-trading assets, in full detail. It should be understood that in Pacioli the entries in the inventory book do not include values (except where value is the only unit of measure as for cash or debts), and that others besides the merchant could make entries in the inventory book or records (" ...che per te o per altri fosse scritto "). In this manner the merchant who kept his own journal could withhold from his staff information about his private assets and wealth.[21]

Ympyn (1543; 1547) handles the matter somewhat differently. In the fourth chapter he advises that the entries in the inventory book or records, which include the values of all the assets, should not be recorded in the memorial or waste-book: " There are some that write in the beginnyng of this boke of Memoriall the Inventory, whiche I cannot praise, forasmuche as this boke commeth daily into the handes of every persone... ". The treatment in the journal is not quite clear. The inventory entries are to be transferred to the journal, " reservyng the boke of your Journall Inventory to be locked in a cheste, that it be not made comon and knowen to all suche as shall handle or write in your boke..." (chapter 10). Thus for Ympyn the journal was not a secret book; and secrecy was secured by (apparently) segregating and detaching the inventory entries. It is not obvious why it was necessary for the inventory details to be entered in the journal at all, since the ledger entries could have been made directly from the inventory itself. In any event, in his model journal Ympyn treats the opening inventory entries the same as subsequent entries; there is no hint of their segregation.

Peele addressed himself in the eleventh chapter of the *Maner and fourme* to the problem " of suche as will have their substaunce kepte in secrete ". The solution is similar to that suggested by Ympyn: " They maye binde their inventorye and

---

(21) In the ninth chapter of Mellis (1588) the journal is said to be " a secrete booke ", and, as in Pacioli, it is said therefore to be safe " therein " to " shew write and expresse al your goods moveable and immoveable...". Here Mellis forgot that in the third chapter he advised the insertion of values of some of the (non-monetary) assets in the inventory, and that values are shown for all items in the inventory in the worked example. He evidently was inconsistent in his modification and augmentation of Oldcastle's original text (see pp. 67-8).

the parcels therof whiche are borne into the Jornall, in the formost ende of their quaterne [ledger] before the kalender [index]... ".

Weddington (1567) was the first to describe the division of the ledger into the secret or private ledger in which the merchant entered all his assets (both private and business), and a business ledger; and to explain how the two ledgers could be made to interlock.[22] "For breviation", Weddington did not illustrate what he described. It was left to Peele, who in this matter also seems to have borrowed from Weddington, to illustrate the use of two interlocking ledgers in the *Pathe waye*: the "great boke of accomptes contayninge my private reconinge..." kept by the owner, and the "great booke... for thaccomptes in trafique of marchaundies" kept by his servant. The superiority and "accountantly" elegance of this method for maintaining secrecy are evident. Peele, nevertheless, also refers to the familiar method of segregating the inventory details from the account-books used or seen by persons other than the owner or his account-keeper. In the set of accounts for the owner's business transactions ("trafique in marchaundise") the inventory is recorded in a separate book, which "must by thaccompte keper, be kept a parte... for that it maketh the stocke or capitall manifest, which is to be kepte secreate, excepte to the master and his accompte keper". The inventory items are not entered into the journal, but are posted directly to the ledger, in fact as a single credit to the capital account, being the excess of assets over liabilities, that is the "net rest" or "stocke". (Peele remarks that the separate entry of each item of the inventory in the capital account "woulde have required thrise asmuche tyme and labour at the least".) Moreover, Peele explains that he places the capital account on the first leaf of the business ledger so that it "maye the better be kept secrete, for that it maye (if a man will) be sewed close with the former leafe, and but be opened at the pleasure of the master or accompte keper".

(d) **Treatment of bad and doubtful debts**

There is no reason to suppose that people were more meticulous and reliable in paying their business debts in the period covered in this survey than in later periods. Yet bad and doubtful debts appear infrequently in the early treatises. One of these occurrences is in Pacioli. In the third chapter, on the inventory, he advises that the entry for debtors should distinguish between the amount of good debts and that

(22) For Weddington's text, see Yamey, Edey and Thomson (1963), p. 36.

of had (" ...debo scotere ducati tanti etc. de bini denari, se siran persone da bene etc. altramenti dirai de tristi denari etc."). But he does not indicate whether they should be treated differently in the accounts.

Peele's *Pathe waye* is the first treatise in which the reader is advised how to deal with doubtful debtors in the accounts. At the end of the opening inventory is included " set aparte, to be kept in minde ", a list of " doutfull detters &c." with the individual amounts, which are not totalled nor included in the calculation of the owner's capital. Journal entries 182–4 record that full or part payment was made of these debts, entailing corresponding credit entries to the profit-and-loss account. The entries in the inventory are suitably annotated for these subsequent events. But no example is given of the assignment of a debt to the category of doubtful debtors.

(e) Treatment of barter transactions

Barter transactions are described and illustrated in most of the early works. The attention given to them probably derives more from their usefulness in illustrating the duality of transactions than from the importance of barter in mercantile business of the time.

The typical bookkeeping treatment was to have a single simple journal entry for a straightforward exchange of goods (or other asset) against goods. One goods account is debited, and the other credited. An example is in Peele's *Maner and fourme*, journal entry 63. A variation was to have two simple journal entries: the merchant with whom the deal was made appears as creditor in one, and as an equal debtor in the other. Both alternative methods are shown in Manzoni (1540).

Where the values of the bartered goods were unequal, the difference could be made up in cash, bills or indebtedness or some combination of these. In the earliest German works such transactions are recorded in single compound entries[23]; elsewhere, in a series of simple journal entries, as in the *Maner and fourme*, journal entries 64–6.

Pacioli was the only author before Ympyn to concern himself with the values to be placed in the ledger accounts on the bartered goods or assets. Barter was an important topic for Pacioli. The arithmetic of barter transactions is the subject of

---

[23] Hübner (1567) flounders badly in his treatment of complicated barter transactions; the author evidently did not understand the purport of the correct entries in his model, Schreiber (1518). Schweicker (1549) is also unsound on complicated exchanges.

a separate short *tractatus* in the *Summa* (dist. 9, tr. 3). It appears in the *tractatus* on bookkeeping in chapter 9 on the nine ways of buying soods (" De li 9 modi per li quali communamente si costuma fra li mercanti comprare... "). And the accounting treatment of barter occupies the whole of chapter 20. In this chapter Pacioli explains that it is necessary to show the exchanged goods at their values in cash (" valere a contanti ") so that the profit or loss made on these goods can be ascertained readily. If other values are inserted in the ledger, it would be impossible to determine the outcomes without great difficulty (" ...senza grandissima difficulta..."). This advice is repeated in the section at the end of the *tractatus* (" Casi che apartiene... "), where the reader is told to value the pepper acquired in barter according to his estimate of its cash value (" ...istima quello che vale il pipere a tua discretione a denari contanti...").

Ympyn (1543 ; 1547) deals more elaborately with this matter. The seventeenth chapter (corresponding to Pacioli's twentieth) is headed " How to kepe accomptes of chaunges, called Barrato in Itallian ". Ympyn warns that " in this thyng is speciall heede to bee taken, for in this maner of choppyng and chaungyng lieth greate hasard and daungier, and no little deceite and falsehed is wrought therin...". He distinguishes between ordinary exchanges (for which the wares involved " must be entred on bothe sides at the marchantes price ") and the bartering he has in mind " whiche is made a purpose on bothe partes, the one to deceive and beguyle the other ". The entries for this type of deceitful bartering are illustrated in the model journal. Four simple entries are required. The barter account (to use Peele's term) is debited to the other party to the transaction for the goods received, valued at the transaction price. The next entry is in reverse as to debit and credit, to record the goods transferred to the other party. The third and fourth entries record, at realistic prices rather than at the inflated transaction prices, a debit to the appropriate goods account for the goods received, and a credit to the other appropriate goods account for the goods disposed of. In each case the barter account takes up the counterbalancing credit and debit, so that as these amounts are equal, this account is balanced. Ympyn explains that by this procedure " ye shall alwaies perceive whether ye gayned or lost by your bartryng ".

Peele adopts this procedure in the *Pathe waye* ; and it seems a clear instance of direct borrowing from Ympyn. Several examples, beginning with numbers 107-8, concern goods delivered or received in " barter at thexcessyve price ". The entries are as in Ympyn, the sole difference being that the third and fourth entries are not recorded in the journal but are made directly (presumably from the memorial) to the ledger accounts, " to avoyde prolixitie ". Peele observes that " thaccompte of barter is not onlye ballanced, but also the goodes receaved and delivered at thexcessyve pryce, are uniformelie charged and discharged, as if they had bene bought and solde for readie monie ".

Neither Ympyn nor Peele considers the case where the merchant perceives that he has made a profit on the barter transaction because the other party " over-paid " him. This omission is particularly surprising in that Ympyn lays so much stress on the use of guile in barter.

(f) Treatment of insurance transactions

Insurance (or assurance) transactions do not figure prominently in the early treatises. They are merely noted by Pacioli. But Peele gives some attention to them in the *Maner and fourme*, and illustrates them in journal entries 84 to 90. The peculiarity of his treatment lies in the fact that the insurer is at the outset debited with the insured value of the goods—perhaps to remind the merchant of his contingent claim on him. A similar treatment is to be found in some continental treatises such as the later ones of Mennher and also in Gammersfelder (1570).

In his second book Peele adopts the more usual treatment of insurance, although he does not illustrate the matter in the form of specimen journal entries. The premium paid is debited to the profit-and-loss account, and no further entries are made at that time.

Peele also considers another question, namely, the accounts to be kept by a person who engages in business as an insurer: " what maner of accompte do suche men kepe as use to asure other mens goodes ". He distinguishes two methods. The first is to enter premiums received to the credit, and compensation paid to the debit, of profit-and-loss account. The second is to have an account of assurances to receive the various debits and credits. From this account the insurer " shall perceave whether he savethe or loseth by delinge in assuraunces, and the difference in that accompte of assurance at ballancing of the bookes, is to be borne orderlie to thaccompt of profitt & losse ". There is no adjustment for any contingent liability on unexpired insured risks.

Peele's consideration of the accounting requirements of insurers is characteristic of his attention in his second treatise to the special needs of particular types of business. Thus he has advice for farmers, and, at greater length, for retailers (as distinct from merchants). He describes the account-books to be used by a retailer, the recording of transactions and the balancing of the accounts. Peele is here concerned with the accounts of an independent retail business with its own account-books. His predecessors, Pacioli (1494) and Ympyn (1543; 1547), were concerned with the accounts for a retail shop owned by a merchant engaged primarily in wholesale business. They therefore describe how the retail activities are to be recorded in the merchant's own account-books, principally in a separate retail or shop account. In his first treatise Peele describes the entries to deal with this type of situation.

(g) A couplet from a verse

The earliest example of a piece of verse in a treatise on bookkeeping is in Manzoni (1540). The thirteenth chapter on the journal is a brief summary, in verse format with some couplets in rhyme, of rules for the journal and ledger (" Regole brevissime del giornal & quaderno "). Peele has two verses in each of his treatises. The second verse is headed " Rules to be observed " in the first treatise; and there is a corresponding but more elaborate verse in the second.

A couplet in each of these verses embodies a piece of advice to merchants and account-keepers which, one imagines, was of the kind given by experienced people to apprentices or pupils. In the first treatise the couplet is:

And to receive before you write, and write before you paye,
So shall no parte of your accompt, in any wyse decaye.

In the second it is:

And or [=ere] ye wright receave, but wright before you paye:
So shall no parte of your accompte in anye wise decaye.

A couplet containing part of the advice appears in Weddington (1567) in the short verse " A good doctrine for all marchantis ":

And alwais writ before ye do paye
That your monni thereby do nat decaie.

The advice appears, in verse form, in some seventeenth century publications. It is to be found in Carpenter (1632) :

> Receive before you write, and write before you pay,
> So shall you be sure your Account shall never decay.

The following couplet is to be found right at the end of Marius (1684), on the one-page " Short Instructions how to keep Merchants Books of Account, after the Italian Method " :

> Receive before you write, and write before you pay,
> And so a good Account, be sure to keep you may.

The same couplet is worked in, incongruously, in a passage in Liset (1684) which was taken without acknowledgement from Malynes (1622).

No doubt the same mercantile advice, whether or not in verse form, can also be found elsewhere. In Larue (1758) the sentiment is expressed in Italian in a French book : " Scrive e puoi paga, Riceve e puoi scrive[24] ".

5. INFLUENCES ON PEELE

In several places in the preceding discussion attention has been drawn to possible or probable borrowings by Peele from earlier publications. Here a more systematic attempt is made to trace possible influences on Peele.

The task of establishing influences is difficult for various reasons, even though the valuable and painstaking studies by P. Kats have cleared much of the way.[25] Peele may have been influenced by practitioners of the art of bookkeeping, or by schoolmasters who gave instruction.[26] We do not know what languages Peele had access to, whether directly or through intermediaries. Again, the subject-matter

---

[24] See Stevelinck, Catalogue (1970), p. 150.

[25] See Kats (1925), (1926) and (1930).

[26] The difficulty can be illustrated by means of an unimportant example. In the *Pathe waye*, when discussing an accounting system for an independent retail shop, Peele refers to the use of a " shoppe booke for sale of all thinges solde for readye monie ". Kats (1925) instances the reference to a shop book as an example of the influence on Peele of Ympyn, although he notes that the general treatment of retailing accounts differs in the two treatises. He observes that Ympyn was the first in the literature to refer to the use of a shop book. But shop books for retail transactions were also used in practice, for example in Smythe's ledger. See Vanes (1974), e. g. p. 118. It is as likely that Peele was influenced by practice as that he was influenced by Ympyn ; the former influence was perhaps the more likely one, since in the English version (1547) of Ympyn the term used is " retaile boke " and not " shop book ", and since Peele's general treatment of the retailing business is quite different from Ympyn's.

itself might have had some constraining effect on the arrangement of the topics and the treatment accorded to them in any well-designed treatise, so that several treatises might bear a strong family resemblance to one another. But not much weight need be given to this last consideration. Peele's *Pathe waye* is, as a whole, vastly different from anything published before it; and his earlier book also has sufficient "new" features, both in detail and also as a whole, to distinguish it from any of its predecessors.[27]

(a) Pacioli

Nevertheless, it is likely that some details in Peele's *Maner and fourme* derive from Pacioli, either directly or through the medium of Oldcastle (1543) or Ympyn (1547). For example, the first chapter in Peele, in which general advice is given to the account-keeper as to what is "nedefull", has some likeness to the first chapter in Pacioli, even though Pacioli roams much more widely when discussing what a merchant needs. Again, pre-occupation with the preservation of documents and correspondence, which strictly has little to do with bookkeeping, is to be found both in Peele and Pacioli. A further example is the statement in Peele's eleventh chapter[28] to the effect that the inventory must be completed within one day (in his words, that it must not "be devided into mo [more] daies then [than] one") parallels that in Pacioli's second chapter, "e tutto ditto inventario si deve tenere in un medesimo giorno". But Peele, as also Mellis (1588), does not give any reason for this requirement, unlike Pacioli who notes that otherwise business will be disturbed. Yet another example concerns the accounts for the merchant's subsidiary retail business. Peele writes in the fourth chapter that the employee who runs the shop should not be treated as debtor for goods sent to the shop "without he consent & agree therunto". This notion appears also in Pacioli (and likewise in Mellis) in the twenty-third chapter.

These are points which, but for the Paciolian example, one would have been inclined to regard it as a matter of chance whether or not Peele had included them in his treatise.

Other apparent echoes of Pacioli in Peele tend to show the originality of Peele.

---

(27) I now believe I was mistaken when I wrote, some years ago, that Peele's *Maner and fourme* was "well within the Paciolian tradition". Yamey, Edey and Thomson (1963), p. 162.

(28) Two chapters in the *Maner and fourme* are numbered eleven. The first of the two (" The maner to beginne a neue Journall...") should be numbered ten.

Two examples are of some interest here. First, in his opening chapter Pacioli says, as expressed in Mellis, that the " first and principall" thing necessary for a merchant is " money or other substance " (" la pecunia numerata e ogni altra faculta sustantiale "). He adds, however, that some wealthy merchants in Italy began their careers without any other assets than their credit. Peele also refers in the *Maner and fourme* to the merchant who starts business without assets, but he does so in his discussion of the inventory in chapter two: "...but he that hath no gooddes (but suche as at his beginnyng, he taketh on credite) nedeth no Inventorie ". The same point is made in Weddington (1567), and the words used by him suggest that he had Peele as his model. The second example concerns the fact that in the early practice of the double-entry system all the information contained in a journal is also to be found, re-arranged, in its corresponding ledger, and that the entries in the two books are cross-referenced to each other. In his fifteenth chapter Pacioli makes the point that if a merchant loses his ledger " by infortune of thieves, fire or water &c " (to quote from Mellis), he could from the journal " againe renew & make another Leager, with all the contentes and parcels from day to day, and put them in the same number and leafe in which they were found in before ". Peele in the *Maner and fourme* addresses himself to another implication of the correspondence between journal and ledger. At the end of the eighth chapter he advises that in the case of disagreement between the merchant and his account-keeper or factor, the merchant should take custody of the ledger ; " and the Journall havyng all thynges agreable therunto, to remain in the others custody whereby there can be no maner of subtletie wrought, of neither part, by any alteracion : for these twoo bookes ought alwaies to agree, as indentures ".

The second treatise of Peele's has in it virtually no echoes of the Paciolian exposition. Nothing included in the body of its text is both surprising (as referring to some minute detail of practice, for instance) as well as being possibly explicable in terms of its inclusion in the treatise of Pacioli or of one of his close successors. The nearest example of a Paciolian echo is to be found near the end of the dialogue between the merchant and the schoolmaster. The schoolmaster remarks: "...and accordinge to the proverbe, whear order is not kepte, ther must nedes be confucion ". The same sentiment is expressed in Pacioli's first chapter, in Latin : " Iuxta comune dictum ubi non est ordo ibi est confusio". Oldcastle has it in his corresponding chapter as follows: "...according to a common saying : Ubi non est ordo, ibi est confusio. Whiche is to meane: there must needes follow much confusion, where is no order ".

Another example of such a borrowing or coincidence is Peele's statement concerning matters to be recorded in the memorial but not in the journal (and hence also not in the ledger). Where money or wares are borrowed or lent for a few days ("for a daye ij. or iij."), the facts are to be noted in the memorial only; and when the loan is repaid, the entry is to be crossed out "and mencion the tyme of receipt at [error for 'or'] delivery thereof in the margent". In a generally corresponding passage at the end of the last unnumbered "chapter" headed "Casi che acade mettere a le recordanze del mercante", Pacioli refers to loans of jewels or plate to a friend for eight to fifteen days. As these lent items are to be returned, the matter should not be entered in the ledger, but only in a diary ("ricordanze"). The same should be done for similar loans from friends. Did Peele get the idea of mentioning this minor topic from Pacioli, or from practice? Oldcastle (1543) in his penultimate chapter repeats Pacioli's advice about the recording in a diary ("put in remembrance") of loans to friends, but does not limit it to short-term loans. Ympyn (1547) also refers to a cognate matter in his chapter 23 on the treatment of "suche thynges as is not mete to be written in the Jornall, nor in the greate boke": "There is requisite also to be kept a Memoriall boke, when ye shall write what thynges ye lend out as hattes, bogettes, males, botes, clokes, woodknives or any other thyng...". But here there is no suggestion that the treatment is for loans to friends for short periods[29].

(b) Manzoni

A possible influence of Manzoni (1540) on Peele's *Maner and fourme* has already been noted: the numbering of the entries in the journal and the references to them in the text.

Kats (1930) drew attention to other similarities between Manzoni and Peele which, in his view, established that the Italian's treatise was known in London:

Both seize the approach of the coming year as an opportunity of dedicating

---

[29] The treatment of short-term loans is one of the twelve subjects which make up the four-page exposition of bookkeeping in Latin (" de ratione librorum tractandorum ") in Cardano (1539): "Rerum vilium et mutuorum sub brevi tempore datorum aut acceptorum nulla fiet, quanquam magni sint proetii, memoria in libris, sed in parvo quodam rerum quotidianarum libello ".

their work to their patrons and are prompted by the same lofty motives in the compilation thereof; the Italian, in order to benefit his fellow men, according to the talents that God has given him, the English author will, according to the small talent that God has given him, apply his study and whole endeavour to profit a common wealth, and if he is compelled to say with Peter: " Gold and silver have I none", the other confesses: " Riches I do not possess". Manzoni had lived laborious days and sleepless nights in compiling his treatise, while Peele assures his patron and the reader that the writing of his book had been very painful to him. The Italian can only write in the simple language (Venetian vernacular) that he had learned from his mother; polished composition must not be expected of him, and the English author does not write with subtle terms of other languages but rather uses such plain and familiar speech as, in our language, he can devise, and both endeavour to write so lucidly that any reader would understand the art at once and he able to apply it.... Both speak of the memorial book but omit to exemplify it. Manzoni uses the letter R (to), i. e. " Resto " to denote balances transferred to or from another folio in the same or a new ledger; Peele teaches the use of the letter R for the same purpose, and if the Italian has an accounting year covering 12 months (1/3— 28/2), Peele's " Maner and Fourme," too, covers twelve months, i. e. from the 25th to the 25th May following.

(c) Ympyn

The specific influence of Ympyn (1543; 1547) on Peele's *Pathe waye* has been noted in respect of the closing of the ledger and of the treatment of barter transactions.

Kats (1925) noted other correspondences between Ympyn's work and Peele's. Thus a change of date is indicated in the journal of the *Maner and fourme* between two lines, as in Ympyn. Again, any blank space at the bottom of the journal page is rendered useless (and therefore a safeguard against subsequent fraudulent entries) by means of a series of oblique strokes. Another similarity to Ympyn is the use of Roman numerals in the money columns of the journal in the *Pathe waye*, although not in the earlier work of Peele's. Having regard to the nature of the various correspondences, it seems as if Peele had made a more thorough study of Ympyn's treatise after 1553 and absorbed more important features of Ympyn's system in his second book than he had in his first.

(d) Oldcastle

No copy of Oldcastle's book of 1543 is known to have survived. All we know of its contents is what we can infer from Mellis (1588). In his preface Mellis writes that he is " but the renuer and reviver of an auncient old copie" printed in London in 1543, " collected, published, made and set forth by one Hugh Oldcastle Scholemaster...". On the last page of the text the reader is told: " Here endeth my Authour, and for the better and plainer understanding and practise of these rules, I have hereunto added a little Inventorie, Iournal, and Leager, as followeth...", and " a briefe Treatise of Arithmetick all together. &c.". Thus the illustrative set of account-books is by Mellis, which implies that Oldcastle's exposition, like Pacioli's, had no such set.

In trying to determine whether Peele had borrowed from Oldcastle's treatise, two difficulties are encountered. The first difficulty is that much of the text in Oldcastle-Mellis is so close to Pacioli's treatment that, in so far as there are correspondences between Peele and Oldcastle-Mellis, Peele may have borrowed from Pacioli (or Ympyn) rather than from the original Oldcastle.

The second and more important difficulty is that Mellis modified Oldcastle's text in places and in ways which cannot now be established. Mellis informs his readers that the " cannons and rules" set forth have by him " in divers places" been " bewtified and enlarged according to my simple knowledge". Thus wherever Oldcastle-Mellis differs from Pacioli (or Manzoni and Ympyn) but corresponds to Peele, one cannot be sure whether Peele has borrowed from the original Oldcastle or whether Mellis has " improved" Oldcastle's text on the basis of what he found in Peele. There are good reasons to believe, however, that any otherwise unaccounted for novelty in Peele and Mellis almost certainly is to be ascribed to Peele rather than to Mellis. Several considerations are relevant.

As has been noted above, the specimen set of account-books in Mellis is by Mellis and not by Oldcastle. It is clear that in compiling this part of his book Mellis drew quite heavily on Peele. As Kats expresses it (1925, p. 172), Mellis's illustrative materials are " manifestly under the direct influence of Peele". Again, there is clear evidence in these materials of borrowings by Mellis from Weddington (1567). Thus the only part of Mellis's exposition of bookkeeping which is known with certainty to have been added by him to the original Oldcastle owes much directly to Peele and Weddington. Moreover, Mellis's propensity to copy is revealed in the fact that the title of his " re-issue " of Oldcastle is virtually the same as the first twenty-five words of the title of Weddington's book.[30]

A further general consideration is that in his borrowings from earlier authors (other than Oldcastle) Peele usually contrives to introduce some modification of his own, as is apparent in several places in the preceding discussion. However, several of the non-Paciolian passages common to both Peele and Mellis are virtually identical in wording and structure in the relevant publications. It would be surprising if it were true that Peele had avoided direct copying when borrowing from others but had indulged in it when borrowing from Oldcastle.

Finally, the nature of the close correspondences between Peele and Mellis itself sometimes points strongly to Peele as the innovator. Two instances are considered here in some detail.

It will be recalled that in the *Pathe waye* Peele has a set of account-books for the owner's business as a merchant separate from the private account-books which comprehend the owner's mercantile interests as well as all his other financial affairs. The opening inventory for the business ledger appropriately includes only " money, debtes & goodes ". After the business creditors are deducted from the sum of these business assets, the " remayne is the net substaunce, stocke, or capitall, by thowner putt in trafique of marchaundise "

In the third chapter Mellis follows Pacioli in that money values are not assigned in the inventory to each of the various non-financial assets.[30] Thus no money values are assigned to various lots of goods, although it is indicated that other details should be included—for example, " I finde in grocerie wares thus many bales of ginger and so many cases of suger marked with such markes: Rehearsing every sort by it selfe with his number signes and waight ". Non-business assets such as domestic furniture and clothes are included. Nevertheless, the chapter ends : " Then gather together the whole summe of your ready money, debtes and goods, and therefrom subtract the totall summe of your Creditours, and the remaine is the net rest, substance or capitall of the owner to be put in a trafique, &c." It is evident that Mellis grafted an inappropriate passage from Peele on to Oldcastle's Paciolian

(30) See Yamey (1958).
(31) For example, the instructions in the third chapter do not mention money values in respect of " rayment of diverse sortes ", " grocerie wares ", " landes " and " cattell or beastes ". On the other hand, for rings and jewels of gold the " value in sterling money estimated " is to be inserted together with descriptive details and weight. The " valure " is also required for plate and for bedding.

treatment of the inventory. This grafting is all the more clear since the term "net rest" used by Mellis is elsewhere also used by Peele as a synonym for capital or net substance.

But Mellis also took from Peele's *Maner and fourme* when dealing with the inventory. The inventory in the specimen set of account-books includes personal and business assets, and money values are attached to each item. The order of the assets is the same as that in Peele's example. This order differs from that in Mellis's third chapter which corresponds to that in Pacioli. Having modelled his own specimen inventory on that in Peele's earlier work, Mellis forgot to amend Oldcastle's Paciolian treatment in the text so as to reconcile text with illustrative example.

The second instance concerns specimen rulings of the account-books inserted in the text.

In the *Pathe waye* Peele's schoolmaster tells his scholar about "what bookes are nedefull & the preparation of them". After some explanation, he says that the inventory and the memorial need not be ruled, "but the maner of rulinge the Journall and Leager shall ensue, to say". The next page "declareth howe everye leafe and side in the Journall must be ruled". The two following pages "declare howe everie face of accompte in the leager or greate booke (lyinge open) shall be ruled, the one for the debitour side, and the other for the creditour". After these ruled pages comes a statement by the scholar: "This I have perused, & understand you very well". We must suppose that the scholar has been studying the specimens prepared for him by his teacher, who then proceeds to question him. The specimen rulings are introduced smoothly and at the appropriate place.

Closely similar specimen rulings (as well as a specimen index to the ledger, which takes up four pages) are tagged on at the end of Mellis's twelfth chapter. The transition from the text is abrupt, and no attempt is made to integrate the text and the specimens. Moreover, unlike as in Peele, the specimens come several pages after the rulings have been described in the text. Chapter 12 itself deals with the different topic of the posting of entries from the journal to the ledger, a treatment which is indeed strongly reminiscent of Pacioli's chapter 14.

Thus, in conclusion, the non-Paciolian elements in Mellis which correspond to elements in Peele are almost certainly borrowings by Mellis from Peele. This conclusion can be applied also to the "Rule" of debits and credits in the ninth chapter of Mellis, which, save for spelling, is exactly the same as in Peele's *Pathe waye*: "All thinges received, or the receiver must owe to all thinges delivered, or to the deliverer". As in Peele, Mellis advises that the rule is "to be learned as well by rote, as by reason". And in both books the rule itself is printed in Roman type to set it off emphatically against the surrounding black-letter print.

(e) Weddington

Likely borrowings from Weddington (1567) in Peele's *Pathe waye* have already been noted. It remains to add that Peele did not take over Weddington's major innovation in the literature of bookkeeping, namely the elimination of the entire journal and its replacement by a series of books of original entry arranged by type of occurrence: the "memoriall, or wast Boke devided into partis, or Bokes accordinge unto thy dowingis".

But even as regards the organisation of the account-books there is one echo of Weddington in Peele. Weddington advises (in effect) that, where there are many cash transactions, the cash account in the ledger should not be debited or credited separately for every item, but that the entries should be accumulated in a separate "boke of the pourse". Presumably, totals would be transferred periodically from this book to the cash account in the ledger. If this procedure were not followed, you "wolde consume your great Boke of marchandize [business ledger] to[o] fast". In an interesting digression Peele explains how, if the master requires a servant to handle his cash transactions, the latter can keep a "chest booke". There are two ways of handling the matter in the master's own ledger. In the first method, the master enters all the individual items in the chest book appropriately in the ledger accounts affected, including the cash account. In the second method, the master peruses the chest book daily, and enters the individual items directly in the various ledger accounts, other than the cash account. The master balances the servant's book weekly. But no entry is made in the cash account in the master's ledger until the "closynge up of the Masters booke". Then the balance on the chest book is "to be borne into the ballaunce of the Masters booke on the debitour syde". (Some further adjustment must have been necessary, but none is indicated.) The pupil had correctly observed of the first method, "Hearein is the Master eased of the payinge and receavinge of the monie but no whit of the writinge". The second method, like Weddington's analogous treatment, also reduces the writing.

6. PEELE'S LIMITED INFLUENCE AND SUBSEQUENT NEGLECT

In spite of the high quality of Peele's two treatises, and more notably that of the *Pathe waye*, they appear to have had little direct influence on any important later publications. A slight instance of a borrowing by Weddington (1567) has been noted ; otherwise, Weddington's treatise betrays no knowledge of Peele's *Maner and fourme*. It has been shown above that Mellis (1588) drew heavily on Peele. The same is true of Carpenter (1632)—this book is indeed composed of borrowings from others, including Peele's *Maner and fourme*.[32]

Although his own exposition and system of bookkeeping are uninfluenced by Peele, Dafforne (1635 ; 1640) has several references to Peele. Dafforne (1635) says in his " epistle dedicatory " that " want of love to this art " (of bookkeeping) in England " is the cause why James Peele, and others that have written in English upon this subject, are known by name onely, & not by imitation ". Later, he refers to Peele's motto on the title-page of the *Pathe waye* : " Practice procureth perfection ". Later still he praises Peele for showing " us the fit ground-work, how to conceal a mans Estate in the booking of his private accounts... ", and laments that his " well-entrances through neglecting age (or disdain of domestick writers, and extolling of foreign) are as strange to us, as though (as the saying is) they were written in Heathen Greek ". There are other references, and also a critical comment, tempered with respect—" I peaceably pass him, in respect of the antiquity of his work, and long interred body "—on Peele's use of the term " repertition " in connection with compound journal entries. In Dafforne (1640) the author refers to Peele's observation that an opening inventory is unnecessary when a man has no assets. And towards the end of the book he writes : " But if this art [bookkeeping] be not well learned, and the matter heedfully carried, it will lead the actor into a labyrinth, as appeareth by James Peele his accompte-straying merchant " — an evident reference to the dialogue between the schoolmaster and the merchant at the beginning of the *Pathe waye*. Dafforne, incidentally, employs the dialogue form for much of his exposition.

Dafforne refers to Peele mainly as if he were an historical personage of a bygone age. And soon he seems to have been forgotten altogether. The next reference to him I have been able to find is in Anderson's early work on the history of commerce

---

32 On Carpenter and his propensity to borrow, see Yamey (1957).

(1764). Anderson says he possessed "the first work ever published in England on the art of Italian merchants-accounts or book-keeping by double-entry". It is Peele's treatise of 1569. Although the "style" is "obsolete", according to Anderson Peele "understood the true grounds and principles of double-entry accounts full as well as some who have written much later"[3].

REFERENCES

(a) *Early works on bookkeeping and accounting (in chronological order)*

Pacioli, Luca: (1494) Summa di arithmetica geometria proportioni & proportionalita. Venice.

Schreiber, Heinrich: (1518) Ayn new kunstlich Buech... Nürnberg.

Tagliente, Giovanni A: (1525) Considerando io...quanto e necessario cosa...el laudabile modo de tenere conto de libro dopio... Venice.

Gottlieb, Johann: (1531) Ein teutsch verstendig Buchhalten... Nürnberg.

Ellenbogen, Erhart von: (1537) Buchhalten auff preussische Müntze... Wittenburg.

Cardano, Gerolamo: (1539) Practica arithmetice... Milan.

Manzoni, Domenico: (1540) Quaderno doppio col suo giornale... Venice.

Oldcastle, Hugh: (1543) A profitable treatyce... London.

Ympyn, Jan: (1543) Nieuwe instructie ende bewijs der looffelijcker consten des rekenboecks... Antwerp.

Ympyn, Jan: (1543) Nouvelle instruction et remonstration... Antwerp.

Texada, Gaspar de: (1545) Suma de arithmetica... Madrid.

Gottlieb, Johann: (1546) Buchhalten, zwey künstliche und verstendige Buchhalten... Nürnberg.

Ympyn, Jan: (1547) A notable and very excellente woorke... London.

Schweicker, Wolffgang: (1549) Zwifach Buchhalten... Nürnberg.

Mennher, Valentin: (1550) Practique brifue pour cyfrer et tenir livres de compte... Antwerp.

Peele, James: (1553) The maner and fourme how to kepe a perfecte reconyng... London.

Casanova, Alvise: (1558) Specchio lucidissimo... Venice.

Kaltenbrunner, Jacob: (1565) Ein newgestellt künstlich Rechenbüchlein... Nürnberg.

Mennher, Valentin: (1565) Practicque pour brievement apprendre à ciffrer, et tenir livre de comptes... Antwerp.

Hübner, Symon: (1567) Ein new Rechenbüchlein... Danzig.

Savonne, Pierre: (1567) Instruction et maniere de tenir livres de raison ...Antwerp.

Weddington, John: (1567) A breffe instruction and manner howe to kepe merchantes bokes of accomptes... Antwerp.

Peele, James: (1569) The Pathe waye to perfectnes... London.

Gammersfelder, Sebastian: (1570) Buchhalten durch zwey Bücher... Danzig.

---

[3] Anderson (1764), vol. 1, p. 408.

It is surprising that Anderson was not aware of Peele's earlier book, the existence of which is referred to in several places, although not by its title, in the *Pathe waye*.

Beckmann (1783), p. 7 observed that from the scanty information given by Anderson about the *Pathe waye* it was not possible to determine whether Peele was expounding double entry rather than single entry.

Mellis, John: (1588) A briefe instruction and maner how to keepe bookes of accomptes... London.

Malynes, Gerard: (1622) Consuetudo, vel lex mercatoria... London.

Carpenter, John: (1632) A most excellent instruction... London.

Dafforne, Richard: (1635) The merchants mirrour... London.

Dafforne, Richard: (1640) The apprentices time-entertainer accomptantly... London.

Liset, Abraham: (1684) Amphithalami or the accomptants closet... London.

Marius, John: (1684) Advice concerning bills of exchange... (fourth edition) London.

Mair, John: (1736) Book-keeping methodiz'd... London.

Hayes, Richard: (1741) The gentleman's complete book-keeper... London.

Larue, Jean: (1758) Bibliotèque des jeunes négociants...tome second... Lyons.

Oudshoff, W: (1833) Volledig theoretisch en praktisch handboek voor het Italiaansch...boek-houden... Rotterdam.

(b) *Other books and articles* (*in alphabetical order of author's name*)

Anderson, A: (1764) An historical and chronological deduction of the origin of commerce... London.

Antinori, C: (1959) Luca Pacioli: Summa de arithmetica..., distinctio IX, tractatus XI... Milan.

Beckmann, J. B.: (1783) Beyträge zur Geschichte der Erfindungen, vol. 1. Leipzig.

Kats, P: (1925) De invloed der Nederlanders de 16e en 17e eeuw op de Engelsche literatuur van het boekhouden, *Maandblad voor het boekhouden*, vol. 32.

(1926) Hugh Oldcastle and John Mellis, *The Accountant*, vol. 74.

(1930) James Peele's ' Maner and Fourme ', *The Accountant*, vol. 82.

Kheil, C. P: (1896) Ueber einige ältere Bearbeitungen des Buchhaltungs-Tractates von Luca Pacioli. Prague.

Melis, F: (1962) Aspetti della vita economica medievale. Siena.

Penndorf, B: (1913) Geschichte der Buchhaltung in Deutschland. Leipzig.

Stevelinck, E: (1970) [Catalogue entries in] La comptabilité à travers les âges. Brussels.

Vanes, J: (1974) The ledger of John Smythe, 1538-1550 (ed. by Jean Vanes). London.

Waal, P. G. A. de: (1927) De leer van het boekhouden in de Nederlanden tijdens de zestiende eeuw. Roermond.

Yamey, B. S: (1957) Early books on accounting: Carpenter's ' Most excellent instruction ' (1632) and other works, *The Accountant*, vol. 137.

(1958) John Weddington's ' A breffe instruction ', 1567, *Accounting Research*, vol. 9 (also in Yamey (1978)).

(1967) Fifteenth and sixteenth century manuscripts on the art of bookkeeping, *Journal of Accounting Research*, vol. 5 (also in Yamey (1978)).

(1970) Closing the ledger, Simon Stevin, and the British balance sheet, *Accounting and Business Research*, no. 1 (also in Yamey (1978)).

(1977) Pacioli's pioneering exposition of double-entry bookkeeping: a belated review, *Studi in memoria di Federigo Melis*, vol. 3. Naples (also in Yamey (1978)).

(1978) Essays on the history of accounting. New York.

Yamey, B. S., H. C. Edey and H. W. Thomson: (1963) Accounting in England and Scotland: 1543-1800. London.

Zerbi, T: (1952) Le origini della partita doppia. Milan.

OLDCASTLE, PEELE AND MELLIS:
A CASE OF PLAGIARISM IN THE
SIXTEENTH CENTURY

Oldcastle, Peele and Mellis: a Case of Plagiarism in the Sixteenth Century

B. S. Yamey

Supposed use by Oldcastle of an Italian manuscript

The first published exposition of double-entry bookkeeping was Luca Pacioli's *Summa di arithmetica...* of 1494, a compendium which includes a *tractatus* on the subject under the heading 'Particularis de computis et scripturis'. During the last 100 years the question has been debated whether Pacioli had taken this *tractatus* (or most of it) without acknowledgement from a Venetian manuscript. Fabio Besta was the leading and influential proponent of the charge of plagiarism. Balduin Penndorf and Federigo Melis were the principal proponents of the rival contention that Pacioli himself should be considered the author of the *tractatus*.

It is not intended here to review the debate in all its aspects. Instead, the purpose of this paper is to demonstrate that no reliance can be placed on one major piece of evidence given prominence by Besta.

The first book in English on double-entry bookkeeping was published in 1543—Hugh Oldcastle's *Profitable treatyce....* No copy of this work is known to have survived. All we know of its contents is gained from another sixteenth-century work, John Mellis's *A briefe instruction...*, 1588. In this preface, signed 'Iohn Mellis Schole-maister', the writer claims that

> I presume ne usurpe not to set forth this worke of mine owne labour and industrie, for truely I am but the renuer and reviver of an auncient old copie printed here in London the 14. of August. 1543

and he says that the original was by 'one Hugh Oldcastle Scholemaster'. Mellis did, however, add an illustrative set of account-books after the text, 'for the better and plainer understanding and practice of these rules'. He also added a short work on arithmetic.

The Mellis text in many places corresponds very closely to Pacioli's text—so much so that Row Fogo, Woolf and Geijsbeek described the former as a translation of the latter.[1] However, there are important differences between the two works. For example, several chapters in Pacioli are not to be found in Mellis; and several passages and sentences in Mellis have no counterpart in Pacioli.

Besta identified and discussed several instances of differences between the two works. His analysis of some of these differences was advanced as a main pillar of support for his conjectures that Pacioli's *tractatus* was in large measure not an original piece of work, and that both Pacioli and Oldcastle had drawn heavily on a Venetian manuscript, of which Oldcastle's version was the more accurate reflection. Besta claimed, in one place, that Oldcastle's text was a translation of the putative Venetian manuscript, and he believed that in turn the Mellis reissue was a 'faithful reproduction' of the Oldcastle text.[2]

---

[1] J. Row Fogo, in R. Brown, *A History of Accounting and Accounts*, Edinburgh, 1905, p. 126; A. H. Woolf, *A Short History of Accountants and Accountancy*, London, 1912, p. 131; J. B. Geijsbeek, *Ancient Double-Entry Bookkeeping*, 1914, reprint Houston, 1974, p. 13.

In places Oldcastle seems to have mistranslated individual words used in his Italian source. For example, the word 'monte' used in Pacioli is rendered literally in Mellis, chapter 5, as 'mountaine', whereas it was used here in the sense of an aggregation or totality. In chapter 15, the word 'casa' is rendered as 'chest' (i.e. cash), instead of as 'house' or 'firm'. The word 'cassa' was confused with 'casa'.

[2] F. Besta, *La Ragioneria*, 2nd ed., Milan, 1929, vol. 3, pp. 369–76. Elsewhere Besta wrote that probably the *coup de grâce* to Pacioli's reputation as an author on bookkeeping was given by the evidence of Oldcastle's book, which clearly was a translation not of Pacioli's work but of an earlier manuscript: *Rivista dei Ragionieri*, vol. 9, no. 4; quoted in A. Ceccherelli, *I Libri di Mercatura della Banca Medici, e l'Applicazione della Partita Doppia a Firenze nel Secolo Decimoquarto*, Florence, 1913, p. 8.

The Dutch historian, P. Kats, was the first to point out that several of the additional passages in the Mellis text were virtually identical to passages in the works of James Peele: the *Maner and fourme . . .* of 1553 and the *Pathe waye to perfectnes . . .* of 1569. Kats was inclined to subscribe to Besta's general conjecture about Pacioli's lack of originality; nevertheless he was doubtful whether the Mellis text could give it any support. In an article written in Dutch, Kats noted that Besta could not have known that Mellis had taken from Peele a number of passages where Mellis differs from Pacioli,[3] and therefore that these passages could be attributed neither to Oldcastle nor to the Venetian manuscript (and, by implication, that other changes to the Oldcastle original may have been made by Mellis). He noted that Besta evidently was not familiar with the contents of Peele's books, although he did refer to them.[4]

However, Kats's observations on the correspondences between Mellis and Peele seem to have had no impact on the Pacioli debate. They were not noted by either Penndorf or Melis, or by later writers (including myself).[5] Perhaps they have been overlooked because Kats made the main point most clearly in a footnote to an article in Dutch. But even in that article he did not *demonstrate* that the borrowings must have been by Mellis from Peele, rather than by Peele from Oldcastle. Perhaps, also, the point made by Kats has been neglected because Kats was much more guarded in a more readily accessible article. In this article he said that where Oldcastle (= Mellis) and Peele 'agree but differ from Pacioli, it is uncertain which of the English authors had borrowed from the other'.[6] There is no assertion here that Mellis was the plagiarist.

In this paper I examine more closely four instances of correspondence between Mellis and Peele, after I have sketched in the general background. In the penultimate section I also refer to another feature of the Mellis book which helps to establish the dependence of Mellis on Peele.

Peele and Mellis as borrowers

Mellis tells his readers that he added the illustrative set of account-books to the text taken from Oldcastle. It is clear that in this part of the work Mellis took heavily from earlier authors, including Peele. Indeed, Kats came to the conclusion that Mellis's illustrative material was 'manifestly under the direct influence of Peele'.[7] Mellis also borrowed from John Weddington, whose *A breffe instruction . . .* was published in Antwerp in 1567. Thus the entry in the inventory for 'lands and rents' is very similar in the two books: in Weddington the asset is a farm purchased from 'one Maister Iohan Hayes gentilman to me and my eyres for ever, after the rate of 16 yeres pourchase, wher unto ther is belonginge 50 ackers of lande'; the sequence is the same in Mellis, except that the previous owner is 'one M. Iohn H. Gentleman'. The closing entry in the ledger account for this asset records the profit; it appears in both cases rather oddly as (in modern spelling) 'net rest and balance of this account'. Again, a writing-down in the account of household goods is in both cases (in modern spelling) 'for so much as I do find at this day to be wholly consumed and worn' (with Mellis omitting 'wholly').

Peele also borrowed from some of his predecessors; and like his contemporaries he did not acknowledge the sources of his borrowings. But, unlike Mellis, Peele never borrowed slavishly. He altered, adapted or embellished the ideas or expressions he appears to have taken from others. All the cases of apparent borrowing by Peele—the Mellis–Peele correspondences are considered more fully below—are such as to suggest, in the words of Kats, that 'Peele was someone who scorned the use of words other than his own'.[8] A few examples should make this clear.

First, in the *Maner and fourme* Peele seems to have followed a pedagogic device introduced by

[3]P. Kats, 'De Invloed der Nederlanders der 16de en 17de Eeuw op de Engelsche Literatuur van het Boekhouden', *Maandblad voor het Boekhouden*, vol. 32, 1925–26, p. 176, n. 5.

[4]Besta, *op. cit.*, p. 394.

[5]See B. Penndorf, *Luca Pacioli: Abhandlung über die Buchhaltung 1494*, Stuttgart, 1933, pp. 63–8; F. Melis, *Storia della Ragioneria*, Bologna, 1950, pp. 620–23; C. Antinori, *Luca Pacioli: Summa di Arithmetica . . .*, Milan, 1959, pp. 7–10; T. Antoni, *Fabio Besta*, Pisa, 1970, pp. 86–7; B. S. Yamey, H. C. Edey and H. W. Thomson, *Accounting in England and Scotland: 1543–1800*, London, 1963, pp. 155–9; B. S. Yamey, 'Fifteenth and Sixteenth Century Manuscripts on the Art of Bookkeeping', *Journal of Accounting Research*, vol. 5, 1967, pp. 64–68 (reprinted in *Essays on the History of Accounting*, New York, 1978).

[6]P. Kats, 'Hugh Oldcastle and John Mellis', *Accountant*, 27 March 1926, p. 483. However, in an article published in the following year Kats wrote as follows '. . . it is certain that Mellis altered it [the Oldcastle book] by taking passages from Peele . . .'. P. Kats, 'The "Nouvelle Instruction" of Jehan Ympyn Christophle', *Accountant*, 20 August 1927, p. 262.

[7]Kats, 'De Invloed . . .', p. 172.

[8]*Ibid.*, p. 176, n. 5. It may be noted that Mellis took as the title of his book the first 25 words of Weddington's title, with one word omitted and one ampersand added unnecessarily. The title of Peele's first book has in it one element of the title of the English version of Ympyn's book (1547), and a hint of part of Oldcastle's title.

Manzoni in his *Quaderno doppio* of 1540. Manzoni numbered consecutively the entries in his illustrative journal (a procedure also to be found in contemporary practice[9]). In the text there is a table ('tavola') listing the various types of transaction, in each case with a reference to the numbered journal entry which exemplifies the type of transaction and another to the folios of the ledger accounts involved. Each entry in the journal also has a description of the type of transaction in the margin. Peele seems to have adopted Manzoni's method; but he improved upon it in that he replaced the table with a long section in which the treatment of each type of transaction is set out (i.e., the accounts to be debited and credited) with appropriate references to the numbered entries in the journal.

Second, in the *Nieuwe instructie* of 1543, Ympyn introduced several unusual features in the procedures for closing a ledger. One of these was to bring together all the remaining balances on the various goods accounts in a single collective account. Its balance was transferred to the final balance account. The collective account was re-opened in the new ledger, and from it the individual goods accounts. Peele referred to this practice in his first book, but did not follow it in his model set of accounts. In the *Pathe waye*, however, Peele described as well as illustrated this treatment. Again he improved on his model. Instead of re-opening the collective goods account in the new ledger, Peele opens the individual goods accounts in the new ledger directly from the collective account in the old ledger—using for this purpose an additional posting column in the latter account, following in this respect Ympyn's practice in his balance account.

Third, Pacioli did not include money values in his inventory book or record, partly because others besides the owner of the business could write in it or have access to it, unlike the journal which was 'your secret book'. Ympyn was the first to show an inventory with money values for each item. But the assets and liabilities are not aggregated in any way. In the *Maner and fourme* Peele also has money values. In addition, however, the assets are totalled; also the liabilities; and finally: the net balance, the 'substaunce of the owner', is shown.

Occasionally in Peele's works one imagines one detects echoes of Pacioli's *tractatus*. Generally these refer to minor matters on which there was

little scope for originality of exposition or expression. But on more interesting matters closer examination shows once again traces of Peele's originality, even when he might have been inspired by Pacioli either directly or else through Oldcastle. Here are two instances. First, in his opening chapter Pacioli explains that a merchant needs three things, of which the 'first and principall is money or other substance', to quote Oldcastle–Mellis. But Pacioli goes on to explain that some successful merchants in Italy had begun their trading careers without capital, and relied initially on the credit which others were prepared to extend to them. In Peele's *Maner and fourme* the same idea recurs, but in a different context. In the chapter on the opening inventory it is explained that 'he that hath no gooddes (but suche as at his beginnying, he taketh on credite) nedeth no Inventorie'. Second, in Pacioli's 15th chapter the point is made that if a merchant were to lose his ledger 'by infortune of thieves, fire or water, &c' (to quote Oldcastle–Mellis), he could reconstruct it from the surviving journal. In his first book Peele considers a different aspect of the feature that the journal and the ledger contain the same information, although organised differently in the two books. He advises that in the event of a dispute between the merchant and his account-keeper or factor, the former should take custody of the ledger and the latter be given the journal: 'for these twoo bookes ought alwaies to agree, as indentures'.

In general, Peele's books, and much more notably the *Pathe waye* of 1569, impress by the quality of exposition and the clarity and comprehensiveness of the examples. Peele strikes one as an author who by 1569 had mastered his subject, had absorbed the innovations introduced by several of his predecessors, and had reflected fruitfully on the problems of exposition. The *Maner and fourme* is a good work, but has its flaws. The *Pathe waye* is very much better. One can concur in Kats's judgment: the second book 'is an important advance, not only on Peele's earlier book, but also on every other book which by then had appeared in print'.[10] Kats expressed this view before a copy of Weddington's book of 1567 had become accessible for study. Peele clearly borrowed from Weddington.[11] Nevertheless, after allowing for these borrowings, there is no need

---

[9]See, for example, Besta, *op. cit.*, p. 350, for the 16th century journal of Zuan Antonio Barbarigo.

[10]Kats, 'De Invloed...', p. 170.
[11]See B. S. Yamey, 'John Weddington's "A Breffe Instruction", 1567', *Accounting Research*, vol. 9, 1958 (reprinted in *Essays...*, 1978).

to question the high quality of the *Pathe waye* and its superiority over its predecessors.

Mellis, on the other hand, was a heavy borrower—that is evident in that part of his book for which he was directly responsible. There is therefore a very strong presumption that any close correspondences between Mellis and Peele are instances of borrowings by Mellis from Peele rather than of borrowings by Peele from Oldcastle. However, it is possible to go well beyond this presumption. Examination of some of the correspondences makes it clear that Mellis *must* have been the borrower. It is evident, also, that Mellis was inefficient as an editor or adaptor of Oldcastle's treatise.

Some common passages in Peele and Mellis

Scope and Arrangement of the Inventory

Our first example of a correspondence between Mellis and Peele concerns the inventory, and is especially instructive.

Pacioli taught that the merchant's inventory should include all his worldly belongings ('cio che se ritrova haver al mondo de mobile e de stabile'), and should begin with those items most costly and most liable to be mislaid or lost. His example of an inventory (chapter 3) therefore includes both business and personal assets, and begins with money. No money values are attached to items other than cash and debts.

In his first book, the *Maner and fourme*, Peele also includes all the merchant's possessions and liabilities in the inventory. For each item a money value is assigned. The liabilities are shown last (as also in Pacioli), and their total is deducted from the previous sub-total of assets, to yield a final sum: 'and the remain is the substance of the owner'. In his later *Pathe waye*, Peele organised his bookkeeping rather differently. Business assets and transactions are segregated from the owner's private concerns. There are therefore two inventories, two journals and two inter-connected ledgers: in this, Peele was almost certainly following a suggestion for the preservation of secrecy made (but not illustrated) by Weddington two years earlier. Peele's first inventory is limited to assets and liabilities in the business, and accordingly is titled 'the inventorie of employements for trafique in marchaundies'. In the text Peele writes: '... and then subtracte the somme totall of the creditours, from the totall somme of money, debtes & goodes, and the remayne is the net substaunce, stocke, or capitall,

by the owner putt in trafique of marchaundise'. A separate inventory, referred to in the text as the 'inventorie generall', comprehends not only this 'saide net rest, or stocke for trafique before spoken of', but also 'divers other thinges', including the owner's 'landes, rentes, anuities, plate, Jewelles, & readie monie, reserved in his owne proper keping'.

We now come to Mellis. In the second chapter Mellis explains that the inventory includes 'all his substance moveables and unmoveables'. In the next chapter a specimen inventory is presented, the order of items being the same as in Pacioli's corresponding chapter. Business and personal assets are both included. Money values are attached to cash and debts and, haphazardly, to a few other items, but not, for example, to the items of merchandise, 'grocerie wares'. The chapter ends as follows:

> Then gather together the whole summe of your ready money, debtes and goods, And therefrom Subtract the totall summe of your Creditours, and the remaine is the net rest, substance or capitall of the owner to be put in a trafique, &c.[12]

It is evident that Mellis, having followed a Paciolian model in the main part of the chapter (probably reproducing Oldcastle here), veered towards the quite different treatments of the inventory in Peele, and tacked on to the original some slightly altered and garbled sentences taken from Peele's *Pathe waye*.[13] What is correct and appropriate in Peele would have been incomprehensible or

---

[12]In chapter 13, Mellis again used a similar form of words. He explains that, presumably after all the entries for the opening inventory have been posted to the ledger, the credit balance on the stock or capital account is 'the net substaunce or Capitall of the owner to bee put in trafique, &c.'. To arrive at this balance to 'make the summes equall, gather the total hereof [debit entries] in a piece of paper aparte, and subtray it from the totall summe of your Creditor opposite, and the rest is the net substaunce ...'. The purpose of the calculation is not clear, but presumably it was intended as a check on the postings to the ledger—since the balance on the stock account should equal the net balance established in the inventory itself. There is no counterpart to this passage in Pacioli. Peele in his *Pathe waye* also has a check on the opening entries in the ledger. A trial balance is drawn up, 'in a paper aparte', to see whether the 'state of thaccompte' [i.e. the ledger] is 'perfectlie ballaunced'. An indirect influence of Peele on Mellis appears to be in evidence here.

Mellis's exposition is rather clumsy. The balancing of the capital account is not described clearly. Moreover, it is discussed before the discussion, in the next chapter, of the ledger entries for the items of merchandise in the inventory.

[13]Kats noted merely that Mellis had grafted this feature of Peele's 'rather thoughtlessly' on to the original of 1543. Kats, 'Hugh Oldcastle ...', p. 484.

misleading to readers of Mellis.[14] Such readers would have got little help if they turned to the inventory in the illustrative set of account-books. For the example includes assets employed in 'trafique' as well as personal assets such as plate, lands and rents, dwelling house and household stuff. Moreover, the order of the items does not accord with the order in the text chapter; instead, it follows the order in the example in Peele's *Maner and fourme*. Mellis here calls his inventory the 'inventory general'—a correct use, obviously taken from Peele's second book.

Rules for Debits and Credits

The second example of a correspondence between Peele and Mellis to be considered here concerns the rule for debits and credits, referred to both by Besta and Kats.

In the *Maner and fourme*, Peele writes:

> Then as touchyng the enteryng of your Inventorie, into the Journall, as the order of this accompt requireth, you shall in eche parcell of the said Journall, expresse two denominacions: whereof the first shalbee the name of the Debitour, receivour, or borower, and the other of the Creditour, deliverer, or lender.

One of the precepts presented in a piece of verse preceding the model journal elaborates the point:

> To make the thinges Receivyd, or the receiver, Debter to the thinges delivered, or to the deliverer.

This is the first appearance in the accounting literature of a general rule for determining the accounts to be debited or credited in the recording of a transaction (assuming, that is, that it was not already in the lost Oldcastle). The rule appears again in the *Pathe waye*, early in the instructional dialogue between the schoolmaster and his eager 'scholler'. The schoolmaster says:

> Yt is a certayne rule to be learned by rote, and also by reason, and is to be practised in all causes of entring percelles into the Journall for the moste parte, which being well understanded, is a greate, furtherance to that which is yet to learne, and thus it is. All thinges

receaved, or the receaver, must owe to all thinges delivered, or to the deliverer.

At the pupil's request, the schoolmaster explains the 'reason' for the rule. He does this in a longish paragraph, by analysing a few simple transactions.

The sentences and passages in question are to be found also in Mellis's ninth chapter, which in its title, but not in all its contents, corresponds to Pacioli's tenth chapter. The first part deals with the marking of the journal, the numbering of its leaves, the privacy of the book, and the requirement that journal entries should be written 'in shorter sentence, without superfluous words, than be the parcels in ye Inventory or Memorial'. Then follows this passage in Mellis, which is not to be found in Pacioli:

> ... But first it is to be noted, that yee know the two termes used in the saide Journall after the maner as is used in the same, which as the order of this account requireth, is expressed by two denominations: to wit, by Debitor, and Creditor, whereof the first is the name of the Debitor, receiver or borrower; and the other of the Creditor, deliverer, or lender. To the furtherance whereof there is a Rule, which beeing well understood, will aide you greatly: which Rule is to bee learned as well by rote, as by reason, which is thus.
>
> All thinges received, or the receiver must owe to all thinges delivered, or to the deliverer.

As in Peele's *Pathe waye*, the rule is printed in roman type, as distinct from the black-letter type which is otherwise used. After the rule comes a paragraph which is almost identical to Peele's explanation of the rule, the main difference being that different proper names are used.

It is evident that Mellis, when working from Oldcastle's Paciolian text, decided at this point to 'bewtify' the original; and he did so by appropriating and cobbling together a piece from each of Peele's two books.

Pacioli's tenth chapter ends with a reference to 'doi termini' (two terms) used in the Venetian journal. The eleventh chapter explains that these two terms are 'Per' and 'A', to denote respectively the debtor and the creditor involved in each transaction recorded in the journal.[15] Mellis did

---

[14]It should be noted that Mellis did not use the word 'goods' restrictively in the sense of merchandise only. For example, the preamble to the model inventory (in chapter 3) refers to 'this my present Inventorie of all my goods, moveables, and immoveables, debtes and creditors...'. And the heading of chapter 14, which deals with the entering into the ledger of the opening items of goods to be traded, begins: 'How the parcels of marchandises ought to be entered and written,...'.

[15]On Pacioli's journal entries, see B. S. Yamey, 'Two Typographical Ambiguities in Pacioli's "Summa" and the Difficulties of its Translators', *Gutenberg-Jahrbuch*, 1976, pp. 156–9 (reprinted in *Essays...*, 1978).

not use this terminology in his journal entries;[16] and there is no chapter in his book corresponding to Pacioli's eleventh chapter. The first 27 words in the quoted passage, however, are derived from Pacioli or from a Paciolian model. Then the 'two terms' corresponding to Pacioli's 'doi termini' becomes the quite different 'two denominations' of the earlier Peele; and the passage from Peele is rendered less comprehensible by the gratuitous insertion of the words 'to wit, by debitor and creditor'—gratuitous and misleading, since the two terms 'debitor' and 'creditor' do not both appear in journal entries in Venetian practice, in Pacioli, in Peele or indeed in Mellis.[17] At this point, after having inexpertly grafted a bit of the earlier Peele on to the Venetian or Paciolian body, Mellis switched over to the later Peele, and took from it material for a long passage, including a substantial paragraph with virtually no modification.

Illustrative Account-Book Rulings

The third instance of close correspondence between Peele and Mellis to be considered here is about illustrations of the ruling of account-books.

In Peele's *Pathe waye* the specimen rulings appear early in the dialogue between the school-master and his pupil, who, as apprentice ('covenaunte servaunt') to a merchant ('for smale wages, but in hope of good preferment and creadite, having as yet very little of myne owne'), had some familiarity with counting-house matters. The teacher briefly describes the various account-books to be kept, and explains that the

---

[16]Occasionally Mellis seems to have forgotten to remove all traces of the Venetian form of entry; see Mellis, chapters 15, 16 and 23.

[17]The words 'to wit, Debitor and Creditor' appear also in the heading of Mellis's chapter 10: '... and of two other termes used in the Leager: whereof one is named Capsa, and that other Capitall, and what by them is to be understoode, to wit, Debitor and Creditor'. This chapter is close to Pacioli's chapter 12. The relevant part of the chapter-heading is: '... E deli doi altri termini nel quaderno usitati luno detto Cassa, e laltro Cavedale. E quello che per essi se habia intendere'. The Mellis 'capsa' appears to be a misreading of 'cassa' (cash) in the original, whether a manuscript or Pacioli. The last five words in the Mellis heading appear to be an innovation by Mellis, or perhaps by Oldcastle. It is inept. The text of the chapter both in Pacioli and Mellis makes it clear that 'cash' is not to be understood as 'debitor', but as 'the chyst or ready money'. Rather, it is said that the cash account in the ledger should always have a debit balance (or zero balance), and could not be in credit. The explanation of 'capital' is as follows in Mellis: '... and by Capitall is understoode the substance of a mans goodes, or his stocke, which stocke shal alwayes bee Creditor, aswell in your Journall, as in your Leager ...'. One wonders what the reader would have made of this prescription. The corresponding passage in Pacioli also is cryptic.

inventory and the memorial 'shall not nede to be ruled'. He then, in effect, shows the pupil specimen rulings. In the book these take up the next three pages, which are introduced by this rubric:

> This page cominge next, declareth howe everye leafe and side in the Journall must be ruled, and the other two sides folowinge, declare howe everie face of accompte in the leager or greate booke (lyinge open) shall be ruled, the one for the debitour side, and the other for the creditour.

The scholar, having said that 'I have perused, & understand you verie well', is then asked to 'utter unto me howe you understand of the same'. He explains the purpose of the various spaces into which the ruled pages are divided. Thus the introduction to the subject, the demonstration and the explanation are developed smoothly and clearly.

In Mellis, the specimen ruled pages come abruptly at the end of the twelfth chapter. There is no introduction to these pages, which in essentials as well as in most of the detail are the same as in Peele. They come after the rulings of both journal and ledger have been described in words (chapters 9 and 11); after specimen entries in the journal have been presented (chapter 10); and after 'the way and manner of bringing the parcels out of the Iournal into the Leager' has been explained (chapter 12). The only novelty in Mellis's specimen pages is the inclusion of a specimen index to the ledger, with four specimen entries in it. This specimen index extends to four pages. It has no heading or introduction. And there are no cross-references in these pages to any of the specimens in the chapters dealing with the rulings of the various account-books or with the index (chapters 11 and 13).

It is evident from their placing and the lack of integration with the rest of the text that the specimen ruled pages were added by Mellis to an existing expository text. And it is also evident that Mellis had taken the new material from Peele.

Besta was interested in the terminology used by Mellis (Oldcastle). In particular, he noted the absence of the terms 'Per' and 'A', or their English equivalents, in the journal entries. And he observed that whereas in ·Pacioli the two sides of a ledger account were designated by the words 'deve (devono) dare' (must give) and 'deve (devono) avere' (must have), in Oldcastle they were distinguished by the titles 'debitor side' and 'creditor side', respectively. As to the latter, Besta was mistaken. For the headings 'debitor side' and 'creditor side' are not, as he thought, integral parts of an actual ledger opening, but are, instead, no more than descriptive headings to the specimen rulings borrowed by Mellis from Peele.

Nevertheless, Besta's discussion is pertinent to the main theme of this paper. He said that these differences between Pacioli and Oldcastle were modifications made by *Oldcastle* and constituted 'the original part of Oldcastle's work', and that Oldcastle in the frontispiece of his work had referred specifically to the fact that he was introducing some alterations.[18] Again, Besta was mistaken. The only preface in the Mellis book is signed by Mellis himself, and the modifications referred to are clearly those made by Mellis to Oldcastle: '... which rules in divers places, I have bewtified and enlarged according to my simple knowledge'. It is more interesting, however, that Besta should have made the point that Oldcastle had made alterations to the presumed Venetian manuscript which he was supposed to be translating. For once it is recognised that parts of Oldcastle's text may be Oldcastle's own original contributions, the text cannot be relied on in any part as being a translation or faithful rendering of the hypothesised manuscript. Hence no observed *differences* between Pacioli and Oldcastle (Mellis) can support Besta's supposition that both Pacioli and Oldcastle worked from the same presumed manuscript, but that the latter did so more closely than the former. Oddly enough, *correspondences* between Pacioli and Oldcastle provide stronger support for a conjecture of their dependence on a common source; but of course these numerous and pervasive correspondences also support the much more plausible supposition that it was the Pacioli printed text which Oldcastle used as his model.

Partnership Accounts

The fourth instance of a correspondence between Peele and Mellis to be considered here involves Peele's *Maner and fourme*.

Pacioli's 21st chapter deals with the 'partita famosa ditta compagnie', that is, the accounts to be kept for a partnership. Mellis's sixteenth chapter treats of the same subject, under a similar title: 'The manner of the keeping of the famous accompt of companie, how it ought to bee ordered in al the 3 bookes'. Pacioli explains that the partner in question can keep the partnership accounts in his own books, or that a separate set of books can be opened. Mellis also deals with

the two alternative methods. Some passages are closely similar in the two works.[19] Pacioli's exposition in this chapter is by no means clear, and neither is Mellis's.

Peele considered partnership or joint-venture accounts in the tenth (misnumbered eleventh) chapter of his *Maner and fourme*. He seems to have done this as an afterthought, in a chapter which refers to the opening of a new journal to replace the one completed. He explains 'howe to charge or discharge your bookes in any accompt, partable for vyages or otherwyse by compacte'. A 'partable' account is opened and debited (credited) for assets disposed of (received) on partnership business. He explains that each partner should have such an account in his own ledger. In addition,

> it is needefull that every partener doo keepe thereof a Jornall and Quaterne, declaryng therby howe thynges have passed or chaunced in tyme of that theyr partable accompt [meaning here, partnership business], wherein they must fyrst make an Inventory, declaryng what eche man dooth put in. Then entre it into theyre Jornall [i.e. the partnership journal], makying eche thyng debitor to theyr partable stocke and bear the parcelles into their great booke of that compact, as you have in this ordre before bene instructed. And then as the reste of your occupyeng in the sayd accompt chaunceth, so ordre your bookes. And at your viages returne or ende of your compactes, ballance up the bookes. And your parte therein as well as that you put in as your gaynes, beare into the Jornall of your principall accompt [i.e. your own journal], be it money wares or debtes, and make it debitor to the partable accompte, as is in the second parcell [in the illustrative journal] bearyng it to your greate booke, whereon the creditour syde of partable accompt you shall fynde your principall answered with a gayne.

This long passage appears as the concluding paragraph in Mellis's chapter, introduced only by the word 'item'. There are some small changes in wording; the wholly unhelpful and confusing omission of 20 words; and the characteristic addition of the symbol '&c' after the concluding word 'gaine'.

---

[18]Besta, *op. cit.*, pp. 371–2.

[19]Kats overstated the similarities when he wrote that Mellis here 'compares closely with the Italian tract' of Pacioli: Kats, 'Hugh Oldcastle...', p. 485.

In one place Oldcastle (or more likely Mellis) misunderstood the original: the assets introduced by the other partners to the joint venture are debited to the 'stocke of the companie'.

As Kats had noted, Mellis refers in his paragraph to the 'second parcel': he slavishly followed Peele, in a manner which must have puzzled his readers, since in the illustrative journal in Mellis the entries are not numbered as they are in Peele; and there is no entry in Mellis's journal involving a partable account. Mellis's borrowing from Peele is evident here in other ways too. Thus it is only in the final paragraph of his partnership chapter that he uses the word 'partable' rather than 'company', or refers to a voyage in connection with partnership.

Further evidence of Peele's influence on Mellis

In two instances chapter-headings in Mellis closely resemble the corresponding headings in Pacioli, and in each case includes a reference to a matter not discussed in the chapter itself.

The first is Mellis's 12th chapter. This chapter deals primarily with the posting of entries from the journal to the ledger. Pacioli, in his fourteenth chapter, instructs how the journal entry is to be cancelled when it is posted: two transverse lines are to be drawn across the narration section of the journal, one for the posting to the debit of a ledger account, and the other for that to the credit of an account. This Venetian practice is not included in Mellis. The heading of the chapter nevertheless contains the words, 'and the maner of striking out the parcels of the Journall' (in Pacioli, 'e del modo a depennare le partite in giornale').

The second example is Mellis's twenty-first chapter, which deals primarily with the calling-over and 'pricking' of the ledger entries against the journal entries, preparatory to the balancing of the books. In his 32nd chapter, Pacioli concludes with the observation that the ledger entries should also be checked against the memorial and any other books kept. Mellis does not have this observation. Nevertheless, as in Pacioli, the chapter-heading includes the following: 'And the manner of examination by pricks, and perusing with the Memoriall, Iournall, and the Leager'.

This is evidence of careless editing. More to the point, it suggests the influence of Peele. For Peele's works discuss neither the cancellation of posted journal entries nor the checking of the ledger against records other than the journal. It is probable that Mellis followed Peele's example in omitting references to these two practices, but failed to alter the Paciolian chapter-headings consequentially. Although these omissions concern minor matters, they serve to provide some further confirmation for the main themes of this paper, namely that Mellis was influenced by Peele when revising the Oldcastle text, and that he was a poor editor or improver.[20]

Conclusion

In all, Mellis took liberally from Peele. The detectable resulting changes made to the Oldcastle text are important. One must suppose that Mellis made other changes as well. The Mellis re-issue of 1588 is therefore not to be treated as an even approximately faithful reproduction of the Oldcastle text. It is ironical, in the light of Besta's views, to suggest that it may well be that the Mellis text is closest to the lost original Oldcastle only in those places where it is closest to the Pacioli text. This is so, because divergencies between Pacioli and Mellis may have a far simpler explanation than that asserted by Besta. They may be changes made by Mellis.

---

[20]Occasionally the corresponding chapter-headings in Pacioli and Mellis both announce something which is not done in the chapter. For instance, the headings of Pacioli's chapter 13 and Mellis's chapter 11 both promise to tell the reader how the index to the ledger can be made single or double. The double index is not described in either book.

COMPOUND JOURNAL ENTRIES IN
EARLY TREATISES ON BOOKKEEPING

THE ACCOUNTING REVIEW
Vol. LIV, No. 2
April 1979

Compound Journal Entries in Early Treatises on Bookkeeping

Basil S. Yamey

ABSTRACT: This article traces references to and illustrations of compound journal entries in accounting or bookkeeping treatises up to Lodovico Flori's *Trattato* of 1636. It is shown that the practice was referred to, discussed, or illustrated earlier and more frequently than has been supposed.

IN his interesting article on the fifteenth-century ledger of Jachomo Badoer, Professor Peragallo [1977, p. 891] remarks *en passant* that until Simon Stevin described the compound journal entry in his book of 1606, this type of entry "is not mentioned in accounting literature." In fact, however, compound journal entries or references to them do occur in the sixteenth-century literature.

A simple journal entry is one which identifies one ledger account to be debited and another to be credited for the event recorded. A compound journal entry is one which indicates that two or more ledger accounts are to be debited and/or two or more ledger accounts credited for the event recorded. Most sixteenth-century texts, and all the Italian ones, illustrate only simple entries. Where necessary, a transaction is broken up into two or more simple journal entries even though a single compound journal entry could have served the purpose. Thus, Luca Pacioli [1494] described the recording of a purchase of goods partly for cash and partly on credit.[1]

... you must make debtor such merchandise and creditor him from whom you have made the purchase.... And after [having done] this, you must make another entry, that is

[make] him from whom you have bought debtor for the agreed amount of money, and creditor the cash or that bank who paid it for you.

Nevertheless, Pacioli was aware of compound journal entries, and this suggests that they were used in Venetian practice. In the eleventh chapter of his *tractatus*, he explains the use of the terms *Per* and *A* in the journal. *Per* always denotes the debtor "whether there be one or several" (*o uno o piu che se sienno*). And *A* correspondingly denotes the creditor, whether singular or plural. A similar reference to compound entries is to be found in Manzoni [1540, chapter 10, on the journal].

In James Peele's first book [1553], there is also an indirect reference to compound entries. But here it takes the form of explaining that more than one

---

[1] The quotation is from the unnumbered "chapter" entitled "Casi che apartiene a mettere al libro de'mercanti" immediately after the last numbered chapter (36) in the *tractatus* on bookkeeping included in Pacioli [1494].

Basil S. Yamey is Professor of Economics, The London School of Economics.

Manuscript received May, 1978.
Revision received July, 1978.
Accepted August, 1978.

figure may have to be inserted above (or below) the short horizontal line in the left-hand margin of the journal to indicate the ledger pages or folios to which the entry in the journal has been posted:

> The other space [in the margin] . . . , with a litle overthwart stroke, havyng one figure or figures above, and also underneth, is a direccion unto the greate Booke of accomptes [*i.e* ledger]: wherof the uppermoste figure dooeth directe to the Debitoure in the Quarterne [*i.e.* ledger]: and the nethermoste to the Creditour . . .

Compound entries are used in the earliest published German exposition of bookkeeping by Heinrich Schreiber [1518], an exposition which is not in a Paciolian or Venetian mold. The second entry in the short illustrative journal is a compound entry:

> On the seventh of February / I
> K1 bought from Hannsen Schymdt 8
> C3 tuns of herring / each tun at 6 fl. /
> S1 have paid a quarter and will pay
>   the rest next Whitsun / he has my
>   signature. Facit   48 – –

The posting references on the left-hand side are, respectively, to the herring account in the *Kaps* (goods book), to the cash account, and to Schmydt's personal account in the *Schuldtbuech* (personal ledger).

Compound entries are also included in Gottlieb [1531], and in Ellenbogen [1537] which is based on Gottlieb. They appear frequently in the illustrative journal in Mennher [1550]. The particular example here is chosen so as to avoid involvement in the peculiarities of the system of factor's bookkeeping set out by Mennher:[2]

> Cash is debtor 9 ditto [*i.e.* March]
> 1 Leonhard Gal is debtor the same day.
> 4 Jan Fris paid me £88.15.7 in
> 3 cash and further he assigned to me
>   [the right] to receive from Leonhard
>   Gal £100. –.–. which he has promised
>   to pay in 4 days   £188 15 7

In 1567, compound entries first appear in an English text by John Weddington published in Antwerp [1567]. The entries in question usually take the form of a long narrative setting out the details of the transaction, followed by the ledger-posting references. In one example the latter appear as:

	31
	38
	42
	21
In the great Boke A	17
	28
	31

In his second book, James Peele, probably influenced by Weddington's recent example, also introduced compound entries (Peele [1569]). The main discussion in the text on the form of journal entries is similar to that in his earlier book, from which a passage has been quoted above. And the illustrative journal includes many compound entries, of which one example follows:

> 00 Reperticion apertaining to sondrie
> 14 accomptes oweth, to James Hacket
>   aforesaid. lxxxxii l. x s. and is
>   in part of. xx. buttes Sackes to saye.
>
> 28 Monie oweth. l s.
> 00 for so much
>   receaved of him.   02.10.0
>
> 09 Sortinge clothes
> 00 oweth. xv. l. for iii.
>   receaved of him at.
>   v l. per clothe.   15. 0.0.
>
> 36 William Jackson of
> 00 Lee oweth. lxxv. l.
>   for his bill taken of
>   the same James
>   Hacket beinge dewe
>   the. xx. of Julie
>   laste paste.————75. 0.0.
>   Somme in all
>   amountes to————92.10.0 lxxxxij. x.–

---

[2] Pointing (*i.e.*, checking) marks are omitted in all examples in this paper.

The ledger folio posting references are displayed clearly. The layout generally is an improvement on that of compound entries in earlier texts. The use of the phrase "Reperticion apertaining to sondrie accomptes" draws attention to the nature of the entry. Peele explains that the phrase "is as muche to saye that sundrye accomptes owethe to some one thing." The word "reperticion" or "reparticion" probably was derived from the verb "repart", now obsolete, which meant to distribute or divide.

Peele, moreover, explains the purpose of compound entries: he is the first author to do so. It is to reduce the number of entries in the ledger, saving effort and presumably space:

> ... Which ordre in some percelles [entries] will do great ease, for happely a man maye bye or sell, at one instant many percelles [parcels or lots] of or to some one man, then by this order of repartinge: there needes but one somme in the margent [i.e. money column] of the Leager, for the creditour or debitour to answere a number of percelles eyther in debitour or creditour as the case requireth.

The extreme lengths to which this economizing procedure came to be taken are to be seen in some surviving ledgers as well as in some later treatises in which the balance account, the predecessor of our balance sheet, consists solely of two equal and opposite omnibus entries, "To Sundries" and "By Sundries." Examples are to be found in Sir John Banks's ledger dated 1672 (Yamey et al., [1963, plate VIII]) and in the second illustrative ledger in Malcolm [1731].

Compound journal entries occur again in de Hoorebeke [1599]. The following example illustrates the method of cross-referring, in which the single noughts serve the same purpose as the double noughts in Peele, to indicate that the counter-entry is to several accounts:

27 By profit and loss of the company
0̅ [partnership] of us three, to sundry accounts for the profit of said company to each for his share of the profit according to his capital, as follows

0 To Jacob Boreel for his ½   £544.2.11.
2̅6̅

0 To Philippe Castel for his 1/4 £272.1.5½
2̅6̅

0 To profit and loss for my 1/4 £272.1.5½
3̅8̅

Sum   £1088.5.10

We now come to Simon Stevin, to whom Professor Peragallo has referred. The form of Stevin's compound journal entries is shown in the following example (the date being omitted), which demonstrates, incidentally, a common treatment in which interest due on a loan is "anticipated," presumably so that the total amount eventually due from the borrower is recorded at once in his personal account:

12 Jacques de Somer is debtor to
― sundry accounts, because I have given him £500 at interest of 10 per hundred per year, for one month, so that the several accounts are:
19 Cash that I have given him the said principal sum of   £500. 0. 0.
19 Account of profit and loss, which is the amount of interest on the said principal sum for one month   4. 3. 4.
                    Sum   £504. 3. 4.

In the second chapter of his text (Stevin [1608]), Stevin deals with the posting from the journal to the ledger. At first he discusses only simple journal entries "because the explanation is somewhat easier." He then proceeds to compound entries and takes as example the first entry in his illustrative journal, which records the inventorying of the opening assets. He writes: "It is to be noted particularly that here I make use of an abridgement not to be found in common practice; this method appeals to me, although I leave it to each to follow his own judgement." The abridgement is that a single total entry is made to the credit of the capital account. The common practice of itemizing each asset in the capital account is judged to be unnecessarily burdensome

> because if I review the entries in my capital account, it is more efficient [*bequamer*] to have before my eyes the single sum [of my assets] than the many parts [of it]. But if I have doubts about any one of these parts, I can find conveniently all the details in the journal.

He then shows the similar advantage of the compound entry where a merchant buys several types of goods at the same time—an example also used by Peele in the expository part of his text when he first discusses compound entries.

Finally, he disposes briefly of the possible objection to the use of such entries that they make checking more difficult in that some ledger entries will not be matched by equal counter-entries in other ledger accounts.

The first examples of compound journal entries in the Italian literature appear to be those in Mainardi [1632]. An example follows, somewhat abridged:

12	To the Community of	
—	S. Geminiano . . .	L 2163.5
12	To the credit of millet,	
—	170 baskets	lir. 1211.5
10	To the credit of rye,	
—	140 baskets	lir. 952

But Mainardi does not explain the use of such entries. A full discussion is to be found four years later in one of the best of the early treatises, Flori [1636]. Incidentally, Lodovico Flori does not mention Mainardi in his paragraph on those "who have written excellently" on the subject of bookkeeping, but he does include Simon Stevin (*Simone Stevino*).

In his initial discussion of the journal, Flori considers only simple entries. He describes the characteristic Venetian practice in which in a journal entry two oblique lines (//) are used to separate the name of the account to be debited from that of the account to be credited:

> The two little lines serve only to distinguish the debtor from the creditor: and to point out that from each entry written in the journal two entries must be made in the ledger, one to the debit of the account of the debtor, and the other to the credit of the account of the creditor.[3]

The sixth chapter, "Of collective entries" (*Delle partite collettive*), introduces compound entries. Flori explains "that a collective entry is one written only once in the journal, and one which contains in itself many other entries from the same cause." Suppose there are many accounts which are to be debited various amounts "for the same cause." If one proceeded with simple entries (*alla semplice*), one would have to have as many separate entries in the journal as there are debtors, and also one would have to repeat the title of the creditor account as many times as there are debtors. "Now to avoid this trouble, and to abbreviate the writing, one makes one entry alone"; and he refers to the two model entries in the text.

The following (abridged) example is taken from the journal which is part of the set of illustrative accounts which make up the second part of the treatise:

---

[3] The latter point, that the two oblique lines also indicated the need for a pair of entries, was first made in Grisogono [1609]: *due lineete a traverso // . . . significando che d'una partida che scrivi nel giornale n'hai da far due nel quaderno . . . .*

On the two oblique lines in journal entries, see Yamey [1976].

In some treatises (*e.g.*, Gottlieb [1531]; and Schweicker [1549]) the two short lines are verticals; in Moschetti [1610] they are longer horizontals.

0 The following [accounts)] / / to house and
36 shop rents . . . in advance for the first
third of the present year . . . , which each
owes . . . for the rent of the house in
which he lives, as follows, that is:

36 Vincenzo Salazar for house no. 1 . . .
36 Vito Bianchi for house and shop no.
   2 . . .
36 Don Cesare Sereni for house no. 3 . . .

Attention is drawn to three points:

1. It is purely coincidental, of course, that the four accounts happen to be on the same pair of ledger pages.

2. In the book itself, in this particular journal entry the oblique lines separating the debit and credit elements are accidentally replaced by the symbol for a unit of currency, the *onza*—an obvious mistake by the printer corrected here in the translation.

3. When the same matter of rents due is treated at a date four months earlier in the journal, there are three separate simple entries. Perhaps Flori intended to show how the same matter could be treated in two different ways. Two alternative treatments in the journal for the same type of "compound" transaction are also to be found in Peele [1569].

According to Besta [1929, p. 402] and Peragallo [1938, p. 85], Flori "follows up Simon Stevin's 'compound entry'." Although they may well be correct, some differences between Stevin's and Flori's treatments may be noted. First, whereas Flori (as do Peele and de Hoorbeke) uses noughts in the posting column to indicate that no account has to be debited (credited) for the collective debtor (creditor) entry, Stevin does not do so. Second, whereas Stevin generally uses the term *verscheyden partien* (meaning several, diverse or sundry accounts) for the collective debtor or creditor, Flori uses the term *appresso*, meaning the following (accounts). (It may be noted that Stevin

also uses the term *verscheyden persoonen* for transactions in which only personal accounts are involved, and once the term *verscheyden crediteuren*.) Third, unlike Stevin, Flori indents the posting references to the individual ledger accounts which make up the collective debit or credit. In this he was anticipated by Peele. Finally, in the ledger accounts Stevin includes a reference to the journal page numbers for entries whose counterentries are collective, whereas Flori rather unhelpfully inserts a double nought in such cases.

The relatively rare appearance of compound journal entries in the early treatises, notably the Italian treatises, is something of a puzzle. Three possibilities may be considered. First, perhaps such entries were not used frequently in practice and, therefore, some authors did not concern themselves with them in their didactic expositions. However, it is difficult to test this conjecture. Early journals seem to have survived the centuries even less successfully than ledgers, so that the origin, frequency, and geographic spread of the practice cannot be established with much certainty. The late Professor Federigo Melis has shown that a Pisan journal of 1399 contains a compound entry; and he has discovered earlier entries in ledgers in the Datini archives which suggest the presence of compound entries in the journals which have been lost. He concluded that "the compound entry was a feature of Tuscan double-entry bookkeeping in the second half of the fourteenth century, indicating a high level of development" (Melis [1962, pp. 421–24, 429]). Examples are also to be found in a Milanese journal of 1457 (Zerbi [1952, p. 381]). All in all, it may be conjectured that compound entries would not have been rarities in practice in Italy during the sixteenth century, although they may have been relatively unknown in England and the Netherlands at the time.[4]

A second possibility is that some of the early authors were so unfamiliar with the details of accounting practice that they were unaware of some of its niceties, such as compound entries. But some of the authors whose treatises are innocent of compound entries (such as Ympyn [1543] and Casanova [1558]) were businessmen or bookkeepers in practice. Their neglect of the subject suggests either personal lack of familiarity with the particular usage despite their practical experience, or else a deliberate decision not to deal with it. This brings us to the third possibility.

It may be suggested that several of the early authors were familiar with the practice of compound entries but chose to use only simple entries in their textbook expositions and illustrations. This would seem to apply, for example, to Pacioli, to Manzoni, and to Peele in his first book, because, as has been explained above, they show awareness of the practice even though they do not explain it or illustrate it. The exclusive use of simple entries could have served to simplify their expositions. It also may have been preferred for other pedagogic reasons. Simple journal entries accorded especially

well with the familiar dictum that for every debtor there must be a creditor: in Pacioli's formulation (Pacioli [1494, chapter 36]), "all the entries placed in the ledger must be double, that is if you make a creditor (entry) you must also make a debtor (entry)." The formulation by Flori [1636], quoted above, is another example—and it is evidently not in harmony with his subsequent introduction of compound entries. The discordance between didactic precept and the practice of compound entries was indeed noted by Peele in his second book [1569] in a piece of verse which precedes his first illustrative journal. It is fitting that the last word should be with Peele, who was the first author to discuss and explain compound entries though not the first to illustrate their use:

And eke in places twaine, of Lidger loke ye set,
Eache percell that in Iournall standes. The first must be the debt.
Which debt shall aunswered be, in creditour alone,
(Reparticions onlye except, where manie springes from one.)

[4] Thus, Stevin states (see above) that compound entries were "not to be found in common practice." The earliest English examples known to me are of the late seventeenth century (Yamey et al. [1963, plate X]; Yamey [1960, p. 640]).

REFERENCES

Besta, F. (1929) *La Ragioneria*, 2nd. ed., vol. 3 (Vallardi, Milan, 1929).
Casanova, A. (1558), *Specchio Lucidissimo* (Comin di Tridino, Venice, 1558).
Ellenbogen, E. (1537), *Buchhalten auff Preussische Müntze* (J. Klug, Wittenberg, 1537).
Flori, L. (1636), *Trattato del Modo di Tenere il Libro Doppio* (D. Cirillo, Palermo, 1636).
Gottlieb, J. (1531), *Ein Teutsch verstendig Buchhalten* (F. Peypus, Nürnberg, 1531).
Grisogono, S. (1609), *Il Mercante Arrichito del Perfetto Quaderniere* (A. Vecchi, Venice, 1609).
Hoorbeke, Z. de (1599), *L'Art de Tenir Livre de Comptes* (S. Moulert, Middelburg, 1599).
Mainardi, M. (1632), *La Scrittura Mercantile Formatamente Regolata* (G. Monti, Bologna, 1632).
Malcolm, A. (1731), *A Treatise of Bookkeeping or Merchants Accounts* (J. Osborn and T. Longman, London, 1731).
Manzoni, D. (1540), *Quaderno Doppio col suo Giornale* (Comin di Tridino, Venice, 1540).
Melis, F. (1962), *Aspetti della Vita Economica Medievale* (Monte dei Paschi di Siena, Siena, 1962).
Mennher, V. (1550), *Practique Brifve pour Cyfrir et Tenir Livres de Compte* (J. Loe, Antwerp, 1550).
Moschetti, G. A. (1610), *Dell'universal Trattato di Libri Doppii* (L. Valentini, Venice, 1610).

Pacioli, L. (1494), *Summa di Arithmetica Geometria Proportioni & Proportionalita* (Paganino de Paganini, Venice, 1494).
Peele, J. (1553), *The Maner and Fourme how to Kepe a Perfecte Reconyng* (R. Grafton, London, 1553).
────── (1569), *The Pathe waye to Perfectnes, in th' Accomptes of Debitour and Creditour* (T. Purfoot, London, 1569).
Peragallo, E. (1938), *Origin and Evolution of Double Entry Bookkeeping* (American Institute Publishing Company, 1938).
────── (1977), "The Ledger of Jachomo Badoer: Constantinople September 2, 1436 to February 26, 1440," THE ACCOUNTING REVIEW (October 1977), pp. 881–92.
Schreiber, H. (1518), *Ayn new kunstlich Buech* (L. Alantsee, Vienna, 1518).
Schweicker, W. (1549), *Zwifach Buchhalten* (J. Petreius, Nürnberg, 1549).
Stevin, S. (1608), *Coopmansbouckhouding* in *Wisconstighe Ghedachtenissen* (J. Bouwensz, Leiden, 1608).
Weddington, J. (1567), *A Breffe Instruction and Manner howe to kepe Merchants Bokes of Accomptes* (P. van Keerberghen, Antwerp, 1567).
Yamey, B. S. (1960), "A Seventeenth Century Double-Entry Journal," *Accountancy* (November 1960), pp. 639–41. (Reprinted in B. S. Yamey, *Essays on the History of Accounting*, Arno Press, New York, 1978).
────── (1976), "Two Typographical Ambiguities in Pacioli's 'Summa', and the Difficulties of its Translators," *Gutenberg Jahrbuch*, 1976, pp. 156–61. (Reprinted in B. S. Yamey, *ibid.*)
Yamey, B. S., H. C. Edey and H. W. Thomson (1963), *Accounting in England and Scotland: 1543–1800* (Sweet and Maxwell, London, 1963).
Ympyn, J. (1543), *Nieuwe Instructie ende Bewijs der Loofelijcker Consten des Rekenboeks* (A. Swinters, Antwerp, 1543).
Zerbi, T. (1952), *Le Origini della Partita Doppia* (Marzorati, Milan, 1952).

THE INDEX TO THE LEDGER:
SOME HISTORICAL NOTES

THE ACCOUNTING REVIEW
Vol. LV, No. 3
July 1980

The Index to the Ledger:
Some Historical Notes

Basil S. Yamey

ABSTRACT: This article examines the discussion and illustration of the ledger index in some early treatises on bookkeeping and accounts, and comments on the economizing of effort and paper in the early practice of bookkeeping.

TODAY, when electronic data recording, processing, and retrieval are commonplace in business, it must seem odd that a few centuries ago the index to the ledger was regarded as a matter of sufficient complexity or interest to warrant specific treatment in some of the most competent of the early printed expositions of the double-entry bookkeeping system. Pietra [1586] and Flori [1636], the authors of two of the best of the early Italian treatises, and the Dutchman Willem van Gezel, whose book of 1681 qualifies as the first comprehensive analytical treatment of the system, all devoted space to the subject of the ledger index.

Their views and ideas and the practices they described are of some interest, especially as they bear on the more general question of procedures and expedients adopted in the attempts made by merchants and bookkeepers to save time, effort, and paper—a general question which has received only passing attention in the study of early accounting, and which is touched upon briefly towards the end of the article.

SINGLE AND DOUBLE INDEXES

The discussion begins with Luca Pacioli's "Particularis de computis et scripturis" in his *Summa* [1494]. The heading of Chapter 13 announces that this chapter is about the ledger and how it is to be kept, and also about its index or alphabet and how it is to be kept, single and double ("... e del suo alfabeto commo se debia ordinare. ugnolo e dopio"). The discussion in the text itself of the two types of index is brief and uninformative. It reads as follows in literal translation and following the punctuation of the original. In the index "you shall put all the debtors and creditors. By [according to] the letters with which they commence together with the number of their leaves, that is, those that commence with A in A &c. And of the double alphabet. And ...". The words "And of the double alphabet" ("E del dopio alfabeto") make no sense, whether interpreted as a separate sentence or as a phrase to be added on to the preceding sentence. There is no hint of the nature of the distinction between a single index and a double index.[1]

[1] Two of the three modern translators into English of Pacioli's *tractatus* omit any reference to the double index in their renderings of the body of the chapter: Geijsbeek [1914, p. 45]; Brown and Johnston [1963, p. 48].

Basil S. Yamey is Professor of Economics, The London School of Economics.

Manuscript received August, 1979.
Accepted September, 1979.

Jan Ympyn referred briefly to the two types of ledger index in Chapter 10 of his *Nieuwe Instructie* [1543]; but for their elucidation he relied mainly on the two specimens which form part of the illustrative set of account-books which follows the text. The relevant part of Chapter 10 runs as follows in the largely faithful English translation [1547]:

> And therunto [the ledger] must apperteigne a kalender, Registre or. A.B.C. made of thesame largenesse that the boke [ledger] is of or litle lesse, entitled in the beginnyng like as the other bokes are, & this maie ye put before or behynde your boke [ledger] at your pleasure. And moste commonly these Registers be made single, but for suche as kepe greate reconynges and countours, thei use a doble Register or A.B.C. the exemples of bothe shall in this treatise be shewed, and if the boke [ledger] be five or sixe hundred lefes, then shal not the syngle A.B.C. do very well: howbeit the doble A.B.C. is used litle of any nacion savyng of the Venecians.

In the model set of account-books, a double index accompanies the first ledger, both marked with the sign of the cross. Each letter of the alphabet is given an opening of the index. Each opening is subdivided, with sub-sections assigned to each letter of the alphabet. Thus, both "Anthonis van Campe" and "Anthonis van Hoorne" are entered on the opening for the letter A; but the former is in the sub-section C, and the latter in the sub-section H.[2] The matter is put succinctly by Pietra [1586, Chapter 36], "For example, if one wants to find Gratiano Speranza, one looks for it under the S of the letter G." And Samuel Ricard [1709] similarly explains, "André Pels &c. in the letter A at the place of the letter P."

The single index, accompanying Ympyn's next ledger marked A, is one in which the individual openings are not subdivided. Thus, both the Anthonis referred to above would appear on the opening for the letter A, simply in the order in which their accounts were opened in the ledger.

Willem van Gezel [1681] has a long chapter on the index in which both single and double indexes are discussed and illustrated (Book 2, Chapter 6). The author observed that it was still the practice to enter personal accounts in an index under the initial letter of the Christian name. He preferred that the initial letter of the surname be used as the basis for the main classification, because the surname persists more firmly in one's memory.[3] He also gave clear guidance on the treatment in a double index of single-word account-titles such as "Cassa" or "Banco": they are to be placed in C.A. and B.A., respectively. (Ympyn had difficulty with his only single-word account. He placed "Caryseen" (kerseys) under C.C.)

Crivelli [1924, p. 30] misread the chapter-heading of the original, as Hatfield explained [1925, p. 211]: Crivelli's translation of the relevant words is—"how it [the ledger] is to be kept Single without, or Double with, its Alphabet." Brown and Johnston repeat Crivelli's error.

[2] Hatfield [1925] referred to Ympyn's model. Van Gezel [1681] described the double index as one in which each letter also contains all the letters of the alphabet.

[3] Because several debtors and creditors might have the same Christian name, Venturi [1655, pp. 34-3] recommended that where a ledger would have to contain numerous names, entries in the index could be grouped by Christian name, to facilitate search. For example, the page for "A" would have sub-divisions for "Antonio", "Agostino", and so on.

Ricard [1709] suggested a different sub-division of entries in the index for the use of merchants with large businesses, especially with foreign countries. Each page should be divided vertically in two, the first half headed with the name of the city or country, and the second with "Etrangers". In this way, one would find the entry for a person more quickly than if all the entries were mixed up ("mêlé ensemble"). Ricard, it may be noted, strongly advocated the classification of entries in the index according to the initial letter of the surname. The method of classifying by the initial letter of the christian name he referred to as the Italian usage ("la maniere Italienne"), "which one could find in Holland, Flanders, Germany and all over the North, in England, Spain, Italy etc." (p. xxxi). He observed, also, that in France one rarely included the christian name.

ANIMATE AND INANIMATE ACCOUNTS

The double index was designed to facilitate the finding of the folio number of any particular account. Other devices were also introduced to this end.

One device was the vertical division of each opening of the index, with a corresponding twofold division of all the ledger accounts. Such a division was first introduced into the literature by Domenico Manzoni [1540] and was followed by Pietra [1586], Moschetti [1610] and Flori [1636].

In his first book [1540], Manzoni did not illustrate the index. Almost all of the little he had to say about the index is in Chapter 8 of the first part of the book (on the journal), which consists of largely unrhymed lines set out in the form of a verse, headed "Brief rules of the journal and ledger." The last four lines are:

The names of the live accounts, in the alphabet, are placed on the right-hand side.
And those of dead things, are recorded on the left-hand side.
By the live things are meant every animate creature.
And by the dead, goods and all other things.

A lengthy discussion of the index is added after the illustrative ledger in the later version [1564] of his first work, and this is followed by a specimen index to that ledger. In the discussion, Manzoni explains that the vertical division of the index—the page on the left of an opening for inanimate accounts, that on the right for animate—is designed to assist the user.[4]

A division between animate and inanimate accounts is awkward in that some accounts fit uneasily into this scheme of things. Both Manzoni and Moschetti include banks and capital among the inanimate accounts, while the former lists a collective account for certain employees among the animate and the latter

includes a similar account among the inanimate accounts.

Pietra's treatment of the index differs from Manzoni's in one interesting respect. Pietra observes that in the index "you will write all the accounts which are in the ledger, except the opening and closing balance accounts (the "introito" and the "esito") and the expense and income account ("la spesa & l'entrata generale")...." The reason given for their exclusion is that, in his system, the entries made in these accounts are not first passed through the journal. No doubt Pietra here had in mind the usual procedure that entries in the index were made when the journal entries were being posted to the ledger: if a particular ledger account had to be opened for the first time, the appropriate entry in the index had to be made. It may be noted that the omission of any account from the index served to reduce the value of the index in facilitating the use of the ledger and also in avoiding the erroneous and regrettable opening of two different ledger accounts for the same subject—as Malcolm [1731, p. 28] put it, "The same Subject must never have two Spaces or Accounts [in the ledger] open at once; to prevent which, and for finding the Accounts readily, the Index is designed." However, in Pietra's case the disadvantages of omitting the particular accounts would have been negligible.

One peculiarity of Manzoni's index derives from the form of the entries in the ledger accounts. As was not uncommon at the time and later, the full title of a ledger account was inserted as part of the first entry made in that account, whether

---

[4] Moschetti [1610, p. 9] explained that the account for "canelle fine" should be entered on the left-hand side of the index, "because cinammon is neither man nor woman, the names of whom alone are to be placed on the right-hand side of the index."

in debit or in credit. The first entry made on the other side of that account might then have the title in a somewhat abbreviated form. For example, the first entry in the capital account is the credit for the opening net assets and reads, "Cavedal de mi Alvise Valleresso de misser Zacharia, die haver. . . . " The first but later entry on the debit side reads, "Cavedal, à l'incontro die dar. . . . " The entries in the index are accordingly distinguished by the letter *d* or *c* prefixed to the name: the *d* for "debitore" indicates that the full title of the account is to be found on the debit side, and the *c* for "creditore" indicates the opposite case.

THE ALPHABETIC STAIRCASE

Both the subdivision of each letter in the double index and also the use of the animate-inanimate dichotomy helped the user to find an account's folio number by closely pin-pointing the entry on the opening assigned to the appropriate initial letter. But how could the user be helped to find the right opening of the index without trouble? The answer, given by Manzoni, Flori, and others was to cut the edges of the pages on the right-hand side of the index book in such a manner that one could instantly turn to the place with the entries for the desired initial letter. Thumb-indexes are so well known to us that they need no description. But evidently it is not easy to describe their nature and construction to someone who has never seen one. Perhaps the clearest of instructions for making such an index to be found in early treatises are those of Mair [1736]:

> Upon the upper Corner of the first Page, toward the Right-hand, write the Letter *A*, and pair [=pare][5] away below it the whole outer Margin (to a Depth of a quarter of an Inch, or the Breadth of a capital Letter) of three or four Leaves, *viz.* as many as you

think proper to allow for that Letter: Then, the Book being closed or shut, write immediately below *A*, the Letter *B*, and cut off beneath it the external Margin of three or four more Leaves, to the same Depth as before; and proceed in like manner with all the rest of the Alphabet. By this means the Letters will appear when the Book is shut, and the Accomptant may readily open upon any Letter he has occasion to inspect.

Manzoni's and Flori's descriptions are more lively if less helpful than Mair's matter-of-fact statement. They both, for example, compare the displayed letters to the steps of a staircase.

SOME ALTERNATIVES

The index was generally described as being a separate book. Several authors explained that this book should be kept inside the front or back cover of the ledger itself when not in use. The quotation from Ympyn shows that for this reason the page size of the index book had to be slightly smaller than that of the ledger. According to Pietra, "the size of the index should be one finger shorter and narrower than the ledger, so that it does not project, having been placed under the ledger's cover."

Both Pietra and de la Porte [1704, p. 92] observed, however, that it was not necessary to have a separate book for the index when there were relatively few ledger accounts. Pietra referred to his own model ledger which, because it has only few accounts, is satisfactorily served by a single-leaf "alfabeto, repertorio o sia pandetta straordinaria." The accounts are listed as in a single index under their initial letters, with the animate accounts for each letter preceding the inanimate. In this method paper is saved, as separate pages are not assigned

---

[5] The word "pare" is used in Mair's second work [1773]. The passage is the same as before, but for changes in spelling and the use of capitals.

to each of the letters.[6] De la Porte explained that the index could be made on the first two pages of the ledger itself "when one is dealing with a business of small consequence, or when there is not a large number of ledger accounts." Manzoni noted that the index could be a separate book or could be made on the opening pages of the ledger. But he asserted that the latter alternative was not in order, however, when the accounts were kept by double entry.

It clearly would have been difficult or expensive to illustrate in a treatise the most "advanced" form of index book, that is, one in double index form and with the staircase of easy-reference letters at the right-hand edge. Manzoni remarked that he illustrated the single or simple ("semplice") index because it would have been far more costly to have had a double index printed. Moreover, several letters appear on each page of his index. The extent of the additional expense of having a single opening for each letter of the alphabet can be indicated by reference to two examples. Ympyn's two indexes occupy no less than 40 leaves in a book consisting of 114 leaves. The two indexes in Peele [1553] take up 45 leaves in a book of 87 leaves.

The texts of both Manzoni and Pietra show, on the right-hand side of a page in which the index is discussed, a vertical column of the 20 letters of the "alfabeto volgare" as they would appear on the staircase as described in the text. It was left to the reader to imagine the rest. Ympyn's model double index, which has a separate opening for each of the 20 letters, has the same vertical column of the 20 letters of the alphabet in the right-hand margin of each right-hand page. Oddly, on the first 11 pages the column runs from A downwards, and from the twelfth onwards, from A upwards.

A touch of realism in the indexes in both Ympyn and Peele may be noted. An opening is assigned, as already noted, to each letter. The letter is printed as a large capital near the right-hand edge. The letter is placed in the vertical position it would have occupied on the staircase: the A is near the top of its page; the U (in Ympyn) and the Z (in Peele) are near the bottom of theirs.

PRACTICAL CONSIDERATIONS

Not surprisingly, there is ample evidence that businessmen and their account-keepers were always eager to adopt procedures and practices which saved time and trouble. Moreover, paper was relatively expensive in early centuries, and account-books had to be ruled by hand. Considerations of expense and effort encouraged the use of space-saving devices and expedients, more notably in the keeping of the ledger (with its elaborate ruling), and presumably especially where the merchant kept his own accounts, as was often the case.

An incomplete list of space-saving procedures includes the following:

1. When one ledger was full and had to be replaced by another, it was a common practice to close the ledger by compiling the balance account, which was thus the basis for opening the new ledger. Among the objectives of the ledger-closing procedures was the saving of effort in opening the new ledger and the saving of space in it. This was achieved by the elimination of unwanted accounts and account-balances in the old ledger by

[6] On the first page of Flori's index to the ledger there is the following statement, "The present index is made in this form, notwithstanding that [different form] of which the text speaks, for the greater convenience of the printing." The index is in very much the same form as Pietra's "pandetta straordinaria," with several letters on each page and with the animate accounts preceding the others.

transferring them to the profit-and-loss account, which was itself closed to the capital account. In this context, the following passage of Mair [1736, p. 89] is of interest:

> Thus when a Merchant begins to trade, his Stock dissipates and scatters, spreads, sprouts, and shoots out into a Variety of Accompts, ... till by this Propogation a whole Ledger, consisting perhaps of 200 or 300 Folios, be replete, and ripened as it were into a Harvest. Upon this the Books are shut up, and the Articles of Stock that lay lately diffused through the whole Ledger, and seemed to possess so large a Field, being now separated from Refuse and Dregs, shrink again within the narrow Limits of the Balance Accompt. ...

2. A common method for dealing with doubtful debts was to place them in a single account of "desperate" or "dubious" debtors. One of the purposes was to save space when a new ledger had to be opened. As Flügel [1741, pp. 98–99] put it, "if one opens new accounts for each of the doubtful debtors, in many businesses a half a ream of paper would be necessary for them alone." (The debts were noted in a small book.)

3. It was common for several accounts to be assigned to a single ledger opening. In practice this economy measure was sometimes overdone, and could cause confusion. Flori [1636, p. 89] favoured the practice, but warned, "One should have more regard for the seemliness and neatness of the ledger than for the saving of paper."

4. Flori (p. 79), like Pietra [1586, fo. 14] before him, described the practice called by them the "crocciole" or "crossola." Suppose the debit side of an account was filled up, and there were few if any entries on the credit side. To save paper, the debit total would be transferred to the credit side, with some space left for any additional credit entries. Further debit entries would then be entered in the suitably demarcated space on the credit side.[7]

It may be conjectured safely that in practice the more labor-intensive and paper-intensive forms of ledger index would have been used only where a firm's operations required many accounts, that is, effectively many personal accounts. Thus, Flori, who was writing about Sicily, explained that the double index was used where many accounts were involved, and he instanced deposit banks and the city administration of Palermo [1636, p. 92]. In many cases, however, considerations of economy of paper must have conflicted with considerations of economy of effort. A page or opening for each letter of the alphabet is obviously convenient, with or without thumb-indexing. It is also more prodigal of paper than Pietra's less convenient "pandetta straordinaria."

Initially, indexes and their construction may have been unfamiliar to merchants. But the frequency with which illustrative ledgers in early treatises are furnished with some form of index does suggest that the use of an index soon became widespread. Where such indexes have survived—and their chances of survival over the centuries must have been reduced when they were made in separate books or sheets—they are as much of a boon to those who study the corresponding ledgers today as they would have been to those whose business it was to use them when they were being compiled.

Terminology

Finally, a note on terminology. Syno-

---

[7] Both Pietra and Flori liken the "crocciole" to a support which sustains the weaker ("piu debole") side. The word itself, no longer in use, meant crutch. In the glossary of terms which Pietra included in his treatise, "crossola" is said to be a support used by cripples; by analogy, when no more entries can be made on the debit side of an account, the credit side is supported by a "crossola", and conversely [Pietra, fo.28].

nyms for index in the early English literature include alphabet, ABC, register,
finder and calendar. Italian usage was as
varied. Pacioli refers to "alfabeto," "repertorio" and "trovarello" [trovare = to
find], and says that the Florentines called
it "stratto." Manzoni refers also to
"estratto" and "registro." Pietra added
"pandetta," and Flori refers also to
"indice" and "tavola." Flori in fact
begins his chapter on the index with an
explanation of several of these terms, of
which a part reads as follows:

And it is called *Repertorio*, because it makes
it possible to find readily the account you
want if it is in the ledger. It is called *Indice*,
because it shows, as if with a finger, on which
leaf in the ledger it [the account] is written.
. . . It is also called *Pandetta*, because it contains all the accounts in the ledger.

De la Porte wrote [1704, p. 91] that
"l'Alfabet du Grande Livre" was also
called "la Table, l'Index ou le Reper-
toire."

The multiplicity of designations for the
index also suggests that the index to the
ledger was in common use.

REFERENCES

Brown, R. G., and K. S. Johnston (1963), *Paciolo on Accounting* (McGraw-Hill, New York, 1963).

Crivelli, P. (1924), *An Original Translation of the Treatise on Double-Entry Book-Keeping by Frater Lucas Pacioli* (Institute of Book-keepers, London, 1924).

Flori, L. (1636), *Trattato del Modo di Tenere il Libro Doppio Domestico* (D. Cirillo, Palermo, 1636).

Flügel, G. T. (1741), *Der getreue und auf richtige Weegweiser* (The Author, Frankfurt).

Geijsbeek, J. B. (1914), *Ancient Double-Entry Bookkeeping* (The Author, Denver, 1914).

Gezel, W. van (1681), *Kort Begryp van't Beschouwig Onderwijs in't Koopmans Boekhouden* (J. ten Hoorn, Amsterdam, 1681).

Hatfield, H. R. (1925), "Pacioli's Summa," letter, *The Accountant* (8 August 1925), pp. 211–12.

Mair, J. (1736), *Book-keeping Methodiz'd* (T and W. Ruddimans, Edinburgh, 1736).

——— (1773), *Book-keeping Moderniz'd* (A. Kineaid, W. Creech and J. Bell, Edinburgh, 1773).

Malcolm, A. (1731), *A Treatise of Bookkeeping or Merchants Accounts* (J. Osborn and T. Longman, London, 1731).

Manzoni, D. (1540), *Quaderno Doppio col suo Giornale* (Comin di Tridino, Venice, 1540).

——— (1564), *Libro Mercantile Ordinato col suo Gionale & Alfabeto* (Venice, 1564).

Moschetti, G. A. (1610), *Dell'universal Trattato di Libri Doppii* (L. Valentini, Venice, 1610).

Pacioli, L. (1494), *Summa di Arithmetica Geometria Proportioni & Proportionalita* (Paganino de Paganini, Venice, 1494).

Peele, J. (1553), *The Maner and Fourme how to Kepe a Perfecte Reconyng* (R. Grafton, London, 1553).

Pietra, A. (1586), *Indrizzo degli Economi* (F. Osanna, Mantua, 1586).

Porte, M. de la (1704), *La Science des Negocians et Teneurs de Livres* (G. Cavelier and C. Osmont, Paris, 1704).

Ricard, S. (1709), *L'Art de bien tenir les Livres de Comptes en Parties Doubles a l'Italienne* (P. Marret, Amsterdam, 1709).

Venturi, B. (1655), *Della Scrittura Conteggiante di Possessioni* (L. Landi, Florence, 1655).

Ympyn, J. (1543), *Nieuwe Instructie ende Bewijs der Loofelijcker Consten des Rekenboeks* (A. Swinters, Antwerp, 1543).

——— (1547), *A Notable and very Excellente Woorke* (R. Grafton, London, 1547).

TWO SEVENTEENTH CENTURY
ACCOUNTING 'STATEMENTS'

TWO SEVENTEENTH CENTURY ACCOUNTING

"STATEMENTS"

Between 1660 and 1715 various members of the Foley family
were engaged in the making of iron, and as a group they were
probably the largest producers of iron in England. The family
fortunes were founded by Richard Foley in the 1630s on the basis of
works established in and around the Stour Valley. Richard was
effectively succeeded by Thomas, who, in turn, in the latter half
of the 1660s began to distribute his productive assets among his
three sons. The youngest, Philip (1653-1716), kept detailed
records and accounts of his activities. Some of this material has
recently been published with an editorial introduction.[1]

Among the records now published there are two annual sets
of "accounts", one for 1668 and the other for 1669, which respectively
cover the twelve months ended 27 March 1669 and 26 March 1670.
This paper discusses these two sets of accounts from the technical
accounting point of view.

Each set is in fact a short ledger which contains various
accounts, incorporates an end-of-year closing procedure, and is
organised on a strict double-entry basis. It is evident that each
set of accounts summarises the myriad of detailed entries in other

---

1.   R.G. Schafer (ed.), *A Selection from the Records of Philip
        Foley's Stour Valley Iron Works 1668-74*, Part 1,
        Worcestershire Historical Society, New Series, vol.9, 1978.
             The Editor's useful introduction to the reprinted
        material is not altogether reliable on the two accounting
        "statements" considered here.

basic accounting and statistical records, and probably served as
a convenient condensed statement of their contents. The two
documents are therefore themselves of interest as examples of
summary accounting statements prepared by and for the owner of a
number of inter-related works, each in the care of an employee
(to be referred to here for convenience as "manager"). It is not
known whether the preparation of statements in this form was common
among iron makers or other entrepreneurs.

The 1668 accounts begin with a net credit balance on
Philip's capital account of £4,702. (All figures quoted here are
rounded by me to the nearest £). The opening assets are the debts
due from the various managers and "last yeares accompt for stock
remayning" (£7,506), the latter being the total value placed on the
unsold products and equipment at each of the works and at the
warehouse. The major debt is that due to Philip's father. The
year ends with a capital balance of £6,881, the increase being the
profit for the year of £2,179. The profit is not in fact transferred
to the capital account. It appears, as will be shown below, that
Philip was not sure how to close off the year's accounts. The next
year's accounts, however, are closed off properly: he must have
obtained advice or worked the matter out for himself.

The 1669 accounts begin with a credit balance on capital
account ("Philip Foley his accompt") of £8,830. At the end of the
previous accounting year Thomas transferred more assets and some
liabilities to his son, Philip, at a price which must have been
lower than the book value of the net assets transferred. Hence,

to incorporate the new assets and liabilities at their book values, there was an increase in Philip's opening net assets as compared with the immediately preceding closing net assets.

Among the other documents published in the recent volume is a statement headed "Stock and Debts belonging to Mr Philip Foley 27th March 1669". This includes the book debts, unsold iron and equipment (including for example, shovels, barrows, hammers, saws, ladles, measures, bellows, carts, hammer beams, riddles and baskets) at the various works and locations in his ownership at the beginning of the new accounting year. It includes the assets under his control during the preceding year as well as those subsequently transferred to him by his father at the close of the accounting year. The total if £68,830, "soe all the stock and debts att all the workes amount unto".

This latter total includes £26,900 of stock (the rest being debts due to Philip, suitably reduced by the occasional debts owing to others), which figure is entered as a credit on the capital account "for stocke remayning at the workes att my entering throughout as appeares". The remainder of the opening credit entries in the capital account are debts owing by the various managers and the cashier ("my uncle Mr. Henry Glovers accompt of countrey cash"); and on the debit side are to be found the £60,000 owing to his father ("to my father Thomas Foley esq. his accompt which I am to pay him for all his stocke and debts att or belonging to any of his ironworks in Worcestershire, Staffordshire and Shropshire") and other debts totalling £3,478. The net opening balance is

£72,309 <u>less</u> £63,478, i.e. £8,830 to the nearest £. And this
figure in turn is equal to the total of "stocke and debts
belonging...", £68,830 (in the statement referred to in the
preceding paragraph) <u>less</u> the £60,000 owed by Philip to his father.

At this point there is an oddity. On the debit side of
the capital account, after the initial debits have been totalled,
the following statement appears, indented:

> there is due to mee that I have in stocke and debts
> (vizt) bad and indifferent   £3808
>
>   good and sufficient   <u>5022</u>
>
>   £8830

This sub-total is not added in with the other debits in the
account.

It is not obvious how Philip could identify the particular
debts or items of stock or equipment which constituted his surplus.
The roundness of the sum (£60,000) due to be paid to his father in
three instalments seems to preclude the possibility that at the
transfer father and son segregated those assets to be paid for from
those other assets which were to be treated as a gift.

The accounts of the various ironworks managers are of
interest. Each of these accounts is a personal account. The debits
are for amounts accountable by the manager to Philip, for example
sales to third parties and moneys received from Philip or his agents.
The credits are for moneys spent by the manager on Philip's behalf,
e.g. works expenses, purchases from third parties and moneys paid

to Philip or his agents. The closing balance, invariably a

debit balance, is the amount owing by the manager to Philip.

A list of debts due to the manager from customers and others

is frequently appended to account for the balance.

   But the typical manager's account is more than merely

a personal account. It also contains a quantitative accounting

of production, shown as an indented statement on the debit side

of the account. The following is an extract taken from "John

Wheeler of Cradeley forge his accompt".[2]

	T.	cwt.	q.	lb.
merchant iron				
remayning last accompt	28	10	2	27
made this yeare	53	0	0	10
received from Wolverley	39	9	3	27
	121	0	3	8
delivered to Hydemill	10	14	1	17
Bustleholme	13	18	2	22
Hales furnace uses		1	1	2
forge uses		6	1	11
sold retayle	72	13	1	7
	97	14	0	3
soe left as per inventory	23	6	3	5

There are no money entries for those quantitative entries which

refer to transfers of materials to other works within Philip

Foley's group; so that money entries are made only in respect of

---

2.   I have omitted some details in the original..

sales to persons outside the group. In the extract above, only
the entry for "sold retayle" is extended as a debit to the money
column, for £1,289.

Purchases of materials from persons outside the group
are shown on the credit side of the manager's account, sometimes,
as for "charcoles", with quantitative entries as well.

There are a few exceptions where some quantitative entries
have corresponding entries in the money column although no external
party is involved. For example, in "Ralph Whytefoot his accompt
of Hubballs Mill forge" 2 cwts. of bar iron "wanting per R.W. to
make good" is debited to his account for £2.2.6. In "Thomas
Lowbridge his accompt of Wildon forge" almost 16 tons of iron
"wasted in cutting" is not debited to the manager's account, while
in the "Hydemill accompt of rod iron" 19 tons of rod iron "wasted
in cutting at 1 cwt. per ton" is debited to the account. The apparent
differences in treatment presumably reflect differences in the
arrangements made between Foley and his several managers.

The individual manager's account is therefore a mixture
of financial and non-financial data, the common feature being the
accountability of the manager to the owner. In this respect the
manager's account - a summary of a year's transactions and production -
is reminiscent of the periodic account rendered by a subordinate
official to his superior on a medieval estate, ecclesiastical or
baronial. But here the analogy ends, because the individual
managers' accounts are embedded in a complete system of double-entry
accounts, and are in this way linked to a profit-and-loss account.

Sales by the manager to third parties are debited to his account and credited to the so-called general account, which is in fact the profit-and-loss account. Expenses paid or incurred by the manager and purchases made by him are credited to his account and debited to the general account. Thus while it is not possible to derive the profit or loss on the year's activities of any one manager from his account, the combined outcome of _all_ the activities under Philip Foley's control duly emerges in the general account.

The nature of the general account is especially clear from the 1669 set of accounts. The opening debit is for the "stocke remayning last yeare", and is the counter-entry for the opening item in the capital account. The other debits are for expenditures made by various managers and others on materials, wages and works expenses, interest on half the debt to the father (the other half being an interest-free loan), and a bad debt written off. Almost all the credits are for the sales made by the various managers and others, and profits from a few partnerships. These credits are totalled. Then follows an entry: "soe remains in stock as in particulars by the inventory...appears to ballance this accompt made up the 26th March 1670". The closing entry on the debit side is: "more to Philip Foley's accompt for this yeare" (£2,166); and there is a corresponding credit in the capital account. (Interestingly, there is an unexplained piece of arithmetic inserted to the left of the page of the latter account:

What Foley did here was to add the amount of the bad debt written off during the year to the recorded profit, presumably to determine a more realistic profit figure, the bad debt having been one that was taken over at the beginning of the year).[3]

The general account is followed by an account titled "The proofe of the whole accompt". This is a sort of trial balance cum balance account, with debits and credits reversed - and thus is in the nature of the opening balance account frequently encountered in the early practice and teaching of double-entry bookkeeping. The debit entries are for "the severall accompts that follow for moneys due out of the stocke and debts hereunto belonging", that is for amounts owed by Philip to his father and other creditors as well as the closing balance on his capital account (£11,051). The credit entries are for the "moneys owing" to Philip (including the balance of bad debts), the closing stock at the works, and entries for the closing stocks of two partnerships. The totals on the two sides of the "proofe" balance to the last farthing.

The general account in the 1668 set of accounts is defective. The closing balance of stock is not introduced into the general account as a credit, and the account itself does not balance.

---

3. It is not possible for the effective rate of return on capital in Philip Foley's business to be derived with any degree of reliability. This is so for several reasons. Philip did not have to pay interest on half of the loan from his father. Inclusion of an interest charge would reduce the rate on the initial capital from the apparent 34.4% to 14.0%.(Alternatively, the profit plus interest actually charged is 7.0% on Philip's opening capital plus the £60,000 owed to his father). Further, the accounts include no entries for the land, buildings and any other "fixed" assets belonging to the Foley works and used in the making and distribution of iron.

It had a debit balance of £5,008, which duly appears as an "asset" in the "proofe", here called "the accomptants accompt". Philip at this stage seems to have realised his error. A further statement is appended: "Soe in conclusion the state of this accompt is as followeth". The closing inventory is added to the total of the debit balances (taken from the "proofe" account), yielding a total of £14,387. This total is then reconciled with the total of what is due from Philip (or the business) to his father, to another creditor, to himself (the balance on his capital account), "and for this yeare". This latter figure (£2,179) is the difference between the closing inventory (£7,187) and the debit balance on the general account (£5,008), that is, it is the profit for the year.

To return to the 1669 set of accounts: it ends with something unexpected. After the final "proofe" account, there is an account headed "An Accompt of tinn Plates". The only entry in it is a debit entry for £55: "I am out of purse on this business to the 26th March 1670". This amount appears, with a similar description, among the "assets" on the credit side of the "proofe". The off-setting credit is to Philip's capital account, where it is the last credit entry. The editor of the printed selection of Foley documents explains helpfully that the matter referred to was an unsuccessful partnership enterprise which engaged in experiments involving the plating of iron sheets with a layer of tin. In the 1668 set of accounts there is an account of tin plates, with an opening debit balance of £47, to which a further £8 was added during the year

in respect of bar iron and osmund iron supplied by Philip's
father and of interest due to the father "per interest stock ult.
yeare". It appears that the new balance of £55 was not re-opened
in the new (1669) set of accounts, presumably in error, because
an entry for "the accompt of tinn plates" is to be found in the
index ("tabula") preceding the various accounts. The omission
was realised belatedly, and the debit balance was re-instated.
The amount was treated as an addition to Philip's capital presumably
because at the time of the compilation of the "proofe" Philip had
not yet considered the experiments to have failed. What is "out of
purse" is not necessarily beyond recovery. The 1669 set of accounts
reveals Philip as a skilled "accountant" and one who should have been
able to distinguish between a loss and an asset. The treatment of
the account of bad debts shows that even admittedly dubious assets
could be treated in the accounts as assets at face value - a practice
to be found also in extant ledgers from the fifteenth to the
eighteenth centuries as well as in treatises.

THE PARTIMENTI ACCOUNT:
A DISCARDED PRACTICE

ABACUS, Vol. 17, No. 1, 1981

B. S. YAMEY

The 'Partimenti' Account: A Discarded Practice

Key words: Accounting history; Italian method (ACC).

Some four decades ago Professor Henry Rand Hatfield discussed several accounting or bookkeeping procedures or usages as 'instances of atavistic survival' (Hatfield [1940]). He noted, however, that some earlier technical procedures had been dropped, and gave as example the eventual omission of the prepositions 'by' and 'to' (from the Italian 'per' and 'a') preceding the debit and credit elements, respectively, in the journal entry. This note concerns another example of a discontinued practice, the use of the *partimenti* account in the ledger, described by the historian, Bonalumi, in 1880 as obsolete (Bonalumi [1880], p. 209). As the *partimenti* account served much the same purpose as the compound journal entry, this note may be regarded as a complement to my earlier paper on that subject (Yamey [1979]).

The *partimenti* account. is not mentioned by Pacioli [1494], and makes only an occasional appearance in the Italian treatises up to 1800. It appears for the first time in Angelo Pietra's excellent work [1586] on the double-entry accounting system adapted for the use of monasteries. In the glossary of terms which appears after the 67 chapters of the book the word *partimenti* is described simply as an account used for convenience in double entry ('per commodita della scrittura doppia'). The treatment in the text, in the short Chapter 51, is more enlightening. First, the reader is told that this account is always in balance ('sta sempre in bilancia'). Zambelli ([1671], p. 54) makes the same point more vividly. Unlike other accounts the *partimenti* account 'never needs to be transferred, because it is an account which does not live; when there is no more room left on its old page in the ledger, nothing except the name of the account is to be carried forward to its new page'. Next, Pietra explains that the account is called *partimenti* by merchants, because often there are large expenditures or exchanges involving several participants ('diversi compartecipi') to each of whom an appropriate part has to be assigned. He also explains that he is discussing the *partimenti* account not because such cases cannot be treated in any other way but because this way of treating them is preferable. He instances the payment of cash for the purchase of two or three parcels of Flanders doublets ('farze fiandresi') on behalf of several monasteries. The *partimenti* account is debited with the whole amount; and the amount is then extinguished by credit entries in this account corresponding to the debit entries in the ledger accounts of each of the participating monasteries and to the 'vestieria' account of the monastery handling the deal. This method involves only one credit entry to the cash account, whereas without a *partimenti* account there would have to be several entries in the cash account. The former method,

---

B. S. YAMEY is a Professor of Economics, London Schools of Economics, U.K.

he says, is 'very much neater' ('molto piu pulite'). Zambelli [1671] makes a closely related point when he stresses the usefulness of the *partimenti* account in avoiding, for example, the splitting-up in the cash account of what in reality is a single payment. Neither Pietra nor Zambelli, it should be noted, discusses or illustrates compound journal entries, the use of which similarly avoids the sub-division in the cash account of single cash receipts or payments.[1]

Pietra includes the *partimenti* account in his illustrative ledger. Two transactions are shown. The second of these records the off-setting entry for a debit to the account of the monastery's parent congregation, in which the latter is charged for the expenses involved in the six-day visit to the monastery of some 'padri'. This total is then divided as credits among four particular income-and-expenditure accounts, including the accounts of the guest quarters ('foresteria') and the stables ('stalla').

Lodovico Flori avowedly based his remarkably good treatise [1636] of Pietra's, and also deals with the accounts of a monastery. The treatise has a short section on *partimenti* in Chapter 10 of Part 2. As in Pietra, the account is said to serve 'per commodità della scrittura'. It is used when one buys something to be divided among several parties ('per ripartire fra molto'). Flori instances the purchase of six pieces of Gubbio silk on behalf of three other colleges and the college which conducts the transaction.

The illustrative ledger shows the entries in the *partimenti* account for one set of transactions. On 13 April the account is debited with three amounts, being outlays for the acquisition of six bales of paper in Rome, to be divided among various colleges ('collegii') which had requested it. On 25 May the *partimenti* account is closed with a credit entry for the total. The balancing debits are to the accounts of four sister colleges for a total of 5½ bales, the paper account ('provisione di carta') of the monastery which handles the matter for a half a bale, and the library account for the share of expenses in connection with books which came from Rome with the paper. Two points are of interest. First, whilst the first part of the transaction is recorded in the form of three simple entries in the journal, the second part is entered as a single compound entry in the journal, with six debits and one credit, the latter appearing as a single item in the *partimenti* account. It is not clear why Flori used simple journal entries for the first part and a compound journal entry for the second. Perhaps it was to show would-be accounting officials that the same type of transaction could be entered in the journal in two different ways. Second, Flori's treatment runs counter to Pietra's statement, noted above, that the *partimenti* account is always in balance. It is unbalanced for the period between 13 April and 25 May, presumably the interval between arranging for the dispatch of the paper from Rome and its receipt in the monastery. Indeed, for Flori's example it would have been more fitting not to use the *partimenti* account at all, but instead an intermediary goods account such as one to be called 'Paper in partnership'.

The *partimenti* account receives by far its fullest and longest discussion in Andrea

---

[1] Zambelli notes, however, another procedure as alternative to the use of the *partimenti* account in certain cases (p. 50). Suppose a transaction involves several debtors or creditors. The whole amount can be debited (credited) to one of them, and then the appropriate parts can be transferred to each of the others.

Zambelli ([1671] pp. 47-50). The practice seems to have fascinated and inspired this interesting author. In places his treatment is quite lyrical — Bonalumi ([1880] p. 209) refers to Zambelli's 'imaginosamente poetico'.

Zambelli begins by saying that the account could aptly be called 'transfer of accounts' ('passaggio de' conti') because 'its office is to unite several separate accounts, or to separate those united' ('L'ufficio suo è di unire più conti separati, overo di separare li uniti'). At this point the author takes off into a flight of similes. The account is likened to a tun which turns several different types of grapes into a single type of wine, or turns one type of grape into wine and grape residue; or to a boat which can be used to carry sacks of wheat supplied by several people to a mill, or to deliver from the mill to several people; or to a glass in which one blends a drink from wine and water; or to a sieve in which one places meal and from which one recovers flour and bran. And the *partimenti* account, just as the vat, the boat, the glass or the sieve, neither retains or dissipates anything that has been placed in it. Zambelli then illustrates at some length the use of the account.

An 'epilogo' is attached to the section on *partimenti*. Once again the reader is called upon in it to use his or her imagination. It is useful, says Zambelli, to imagine that each transaction which has to be recorded is like a rope with two ends, one right and one left, which have to be inserted into two holes of appropriate size. An end may be divided or separated into two or more strands. If it were so divided, it would not be able to enter its appointed hole. It would then be necessary to tie the strands together, so that the end could be inserted into its hole. The *partimenti* account serves a similar purpose in bookkeeping.

Zambelli, while eloquent on the usefulness of the *partimenti* account in his main discussion of the practice, nevertheless elsewhere in his book (p. 28) expresses strong disapproval of the use by many merchants of this account for recording dealings in which several different kinds of merchandise are bought or sold together in a single transaction. He says the use of the *partimenti* account here is evidently excessive ('soverchio'), even detrimental ('schifevole', literally, disgusting). No clear explanation is given why this is bad practice, except for the observation that one should avoid the proliferation of entries associated with that account. Incidentally, it may be that it was this deprecatory passage which caused Cerboni to write that Zambelli castigates ('flagella') the use of the *partimenti* account (Cerboni [1907], p. 232). He presumably was unaware of the later more favourable discussion.

Zambelli observes that sometimes several creditors (credit entries) as well as several debtors may arise from a single transaction. Then one had double - *partimenti* ('partimenti a doppio'). Again, Zambelli cannot resist a simile (although he avoids the simile of a rope with both ends divided). *Partimenti a doppio* is like a river which receives water from several sources, and then divides itself into several streams. Zambelli illustrates both simple and double *partimenti* entries in his illustrative ledger.

Partimenti accounts appear once again in Vergani [1781]. This book, which has a confused publishing history, consists wholly of a detailed illustrative set of account books and some ancillary financial statements. In the ledger there is a *partimenti* account for taking care of cases where there are either several credit elements or several debit elements. There is, however, a separate account called *partimenti de partimenti*, for cases

5

where there are both several debit elements and also several credit elements. Here Vergani first enters the total sum involved on each side of the account. For example, his second transaction relates to the receipt of silk and hay from one Pietro Morosi in exchange for wheat and a cash payment. The whole sum involved, 335 lire, is first both debited and credited to *partimenti de partimenti*. The account is then credited with 190 for the silk and 145 for the hay; and debited with 135 for the wheat, and 200 for the cash paid.

Were *partimenti* accounts used in practice? No such account has been noted in a surviving ledger. But the fact that such authors as Pietra, Flori and Vergani used them may be taken as evidence that they were used in practice, because it is clear from their works that they were knowledgeable about the world of business and accounting. Further, Zambelli writes, as has been noted, that many merchants were in the habit of passing purchases and sales of collections of different kinds of merchandise through the *partimenti* account. This may be an exaggeration. However, it is unlikely that an author of an expository treatise on accounting would invent a procedure or an account of this kind.[2] Nevertheless, the use of *partimenti* accounts would have declined once the use of compound journal entries had become common practice. Such journal entries can do what a *partimenti* account does, and have the virtue of saving ledger space because no special ledger account is required.

The inference that accounts like the *partimenti* were used in practice is reinforced by the fact that the earliest reference in the literature to an account with the same function is in Weddington [1567], a treatise in English, published in Antwerp. According to surviving records John Weddington was experienced in accounts and business, and worked in Antwerp for several years (De Groote [1978]). His illustrative ledger has an account which serves the same purpose as a *partimenti* account, although it is used only for transactions made in conjunction with others. The account is titled 'the accompt in mount, I saye the accompt for the devizion of all accomptis partable withe me, and other men &c here in Andwarpe . . .'. The last of three sets of entries in the account is taken as an example of its contents. The account in mount is debited for the amount due to Gillis Vermeullen, 'marchant of Andwarpe', for 10 numbered bags of dry pepper. The same total is off-set on the credit side by three entries: one for three bags held by the merchant, Thomas Lane, on behalf of Johan Ede; another for two bags held by Lane on behalf of William Foster; and the third for five bags kept by Lane on his own account.

The word 'mount' in the title of the account was probably derived from the Italian word 'monte'. One of its uses in the form 'in monte' had the meaning 'in total' or 'in one amount'.[3] The use by Weddington of the word 'mount' in the context also suggests that he had encountered the procedure in practice in Antwerp, since Italian merchants were active in the Low Countries and Italian business terms were commonly used.

---

[2] That Zambelli had encountered the use of the *partimenti* account in practice is further suggested by the inclusion in his section on errors of two kinds of possible error in the making of entries in that account (p. 74).

[3] Edler ([1934] p. 189). Edler records another meaning of 'in monte', namely that of 'in bulk'.

REFERENCES

Bonalumi, F. A., *Sulla Svolgimento de Pensiero Computistico in Italia*, Novara 1880.

Cerboni, G., 'Elenco Cronologico degli Scrittori di Ragioneria' in G. Massa, *Trattato Completo di Ragioneria*, Vol. 12, Milan 1907.

De Groote, H. L. V., 'Two Sixteenth Century Accountants' in B. S. Yamey (ed.), *The Historical Development of Accounting: A Selection of Papers*, New York 1978.

Edler, F., *Glossary of Mediaeval Terms of Business: Italian Series 1200-1600*, Cambridge, Mass. 1934.

Flori, L., *Trattato del Tenere il Libro Doppio Domestico . . .*, Palermo 1636.

Hatfield, H. R., 'Accounting Trivia', *The Accounting Review*, September 1940.

Pacioli, L., *Summa di Arithmetica . . .*, Venice 1494.

Pietra, A., *Indrizzo degli Economi . . .*, Mantua 1586.

Vergani, C. G., *Pratica della Scrittura Doppia Economica*, 3rd edn, Milan 1781.

Weddington, J., *A Breffe Instruction . . .*, Antwerp 1567.

Yamey, B. S., 'Compound Journal Entries in Early Treatises on Bookkeeping', *The Accounting Review*, April 1979.

Zambelli, A., *Il Ragionato . . .*, Milan 1671.

THE USE OF ITALIAN WORDS
IN BOOKKEEPING:
GERMANY, 1400 TO 1800

1

The use of Italian or Italianate words was common in early German mercantile accounting. The following examples can be gleaned from surviving records of the fifteenth and sixteenth centuries: *adi, repetitio, debitori, creditori, ultimo, summa, konto (conto), conto aparte, zornal, dato, quaderni, netto, saldo, agio, anno, primo, kapital, kassa, partida, ditto, summa summarum, bilanz, compagnie, pro resto* and *percento*. Moreover, the abbreviation *ac* is often to be found preceding numerals entered in ledger posting columns. The abbreviation stands for "a carta", that is "on page" or "on folio", and precedes the number of the page or folio referred to. The same abbreviation is to be found in some early Italian account-books, and also in Pacioli's treatise of 1494.

The use of Italian words was not limited to Germany. The sixteenth-century ledger of a Dutch partnership has the familiar *adi, anno, resto* and *billance*, and also *voiage, stilo veteri* and *stilo novo*. (Ten Have, 1933, pp.270 *et seq.*). In the illustrative ledger in Ympyn's *Nieuwe instructie* (1543) the abbreviation *ac* appears. The common use of Italian and other foreign words by Dutch book-keepers and merchants is evident also from a statement by Simon Stevin in his famous *Vorstelicke bouckhouding op de Italiaensche wyse* (1607). Stevin was a strong and influential advocate of the use of Dutch instead of Latin in scientific writings, and he

practised what he preached. However, in his exposition of book-
keeping and accounts he nevertheless used several "undutch"
(*onduytsche*) words, such as "Debet, Credit, Debiteur, Crediteur,
Balance, Iornael, Finance, Domeine". He explained that he used
such words because his pupil, Prince Maurice, wished to apply the
mercantile system of bookkeeping (double entry) to the affairs of
his princely domains. For this purpose he would need the services
of the most experienced and capable bookkeepers he could find.
These persons were accustomed to the undutch words, as also were
others with whom one would want to discuss bookkeeping matters.
The use of newly-minted Dutch equivalents for the undutch terms
would have created difficulties right at the outset. About a
century later de Graaf (1693) expressed a similar sentiment. He
explained in his introductory remarks to the reader that "we have
followed the style and also the words used by merchants, so that
one is not a stranger when one enters their counting-houses". He
added:"The bastard words, however, [are] for the most part obscure".

Johann Beckmann, an early writer on the history of
inventions (1783) observed:

> The designation, Italian bookkeeping, *doppia scrittura*
> and the many terms of art of Italian origin used in
> bookkeeping, and which are still retained in all languages,
> make it likely that the invention [of double entry]
> belongs to the Italians, and that foreigners acquired
> their knowledge of double entry in Italian counting-houses,
> when trade with the East still passed through Italy, just
> as they also acquired knowledge of the so-called Italian
> *Praktik*, that is commercial arithmetic with numerous
> abridgements [i.e. short-cut methods].

A few years later an English author, Patrick Kelly (1801) noted, that "none of the technical terms of Double Entry are to be found in the ancient languages, but appear immediately derived from the Italian, as adopted in the other languages of Europe".

Italian words proliferate in certain German treatises. These words are emphasized in some German treatises in which they (and other foreign words) are printed in Roman type, and so stand out clearly against the rest of the text printed in Gothic black letter. Examples of such works include Goessens (1594), Hager (1660), Marperger (1718) and Flügel (1781). The latter work, for example, distinguishes several types of personal accounts, including *conto suo (mio)* or *suo (mio) conto corrente, suo (mio) conto di tempo, conto di deposito, suo (mio) conto di commissione, suo (mio) conto di compagnia, conto a meta* and *conto per diversi.*

The use of Italian words can be readily explained in terms of the earlier development of bookkeeping in medieval Italy than elsewhere, and of the prestige of the Italian double-entry system.

Andreas Wagner (1801), however, gave a different reason why German bookkeepers and writers of treatises on bookkeeping were prone to use Italian and other foreign terms even in the eighteenth century when the German language was being cleansed of foreign words:

> The majority of works [on mercantile subjects], especially those on bookkeeping, teem with Italian and French words, frequently wrongly spelt. It was believed that one's books were elegantly kept in authentic double entry if in each line appeared *Conto mio, Conto loro à tempo, Conto metà, Conto a terzo, Conto pro diversi,* etc.

Wagner, nevertheless, used several Italian words in his
own treatises. For this he was duly reprimanded by Christian
Hingstedt (1804). The fourth chapter of Hingstedt's unusual
book presents examples of the fashion for Italian, culled from
Wagner and other good contemporary texts. In each case he gave
the preferable German equivalent. "These are the improvements
in language which are recommended to bookkeepers employing the
double-entry method, and which already are actually being used
by several practising bookkeepers here" in Hamburg. Hingstedt
was also critical of Wagner's statement that "each entry [Post]
in which the debtor is given together with its corresponding
creditor is called a *partite*". "I bet that this term is unknown
to almost all bookkeepers in Hamburg". According to Hingstedt,
they were also ignorant of Wagner's use of the word "charta"
(*carta*) in the sense of a ledger-opening of two facing pages
treated and numbered as one.

2.

The use of Italian and other foreign terms in bookkeeping
circles in Germany as well as in treatises prompted some authors
to provide glossaries for their readers who would have included
beginners among their number. Matthäus Schwarz had a list, with
a later appendix, in his manuscript exposition of 1516. The words
include bookkeeping terms such as *debitor, creditor, scontro, conto
de tempo* and *conto de corrente,* and mercantile terms used in

connection with bills of exchange such as *tratto, rimesso, acception* and *protestation* (Weitnauer, 1931). Schreiber (n.d., 1521?) produced no list. But he wrote that one can keep one's books in any language ("though one seldom keeps books in Latin"). He said that several Italian words were in use (presumably in Germany), such as "adi, that is on the day, conto, that is account". The printer of Schweicker's book of 1549 included a short glossary in his remarks to the reader. "However, because various Italian words are used in bookkeeping, which are understood by all businessmen and are used daily by merchants, but which are not translated into German, I have considered it would be useful to give a short explanation of these words and a translation". The words include *cavedal, inventarium, cassa, post, sporco* and *saldieren*. Shortly afterwards Mennher, a German who settled in Antwerp, added the following sentence (with punctuation modified here) after his illustrative account-books (1550): "Since the first invention of bookkeeping is due to the Italians, I did not wish to change certain short words they use, as adj [adi], that is to say, the day; dito, aforesaid; tarra for subtract; netto, net; sporco, with the tarra [=tare]; cioe, that is to say; cassa, money; capital, all the wealth...".

Passchier Goessens concluded his book (1594) with a list of 36 Italian words used in his illustrative account-books, with explanations in German. Several are bookkeeping terms, such as *conto ditto* (the aforesaid account). Others are Italian words used in commercial circles, for example *a monte, compagnia* and *per cento al anno*, or particular kinds of merchandise.

      Hager (1660) also provided a glossary of foreign words for the guidance of his readers, leaving it to them to use the words if they so pleased. He explained that the practice of using foreign words was not peculiar to merchants. He noted that mathematicians used foreign words, knowing that they were familiar, had been adopted for use in German, and were convenient and clear. His glossary, arranged alphabetically by initial letter, contains over 150 entries, many of them used in bookkeeping records. Here is a selection of terms with translations:

adi	von Tage
cassa	bahre Gelder
charta	die Seyte eines Blatts
debitor	ein Schüldner/oder Käuffer
danno	Verlust
factor	Handelsverwalter
inventarium	ein Verzeichnusz der bahren Gelder/Güter/ Schulden und Gegenschulden
partyda	eine Post
remittiren	Gelder auff Wechsel geben
stylo veteri	nachm Alten Calender
voyage	eine Reise

3.

Until the beginning of the nineteenth century double-entry bookkeeping was almost universally referred to in Europe (except in Italy) as the Italian method or system. Thereafter this designation appears gradually to have fallen out of favour. It is unusual to find the word "Italian" in the titles of books on bookkeeping published in and after the 1850s. The reasons for the discontinuance of the adjective are not clear, but two may be suggested. First, it is possible that the arrangement of double-entry records and the form of entries had changed so much from those set out in the early treatises that the method itself no longer was thought of as "Italian" although it still was double entry. A hint of this is to be found in Hingstedt (1804):

> This method is also called Italian bookkeeping, because it was invented in Italy or came from there to us. I do not however see why it still retains this description, as the expression "double-entry bookkeeping" gives the correct idea of the subject, and the method certainly owes its greatest perfection to the German commercial cities - indeed, the method and whatever of it may have come from Italy to us probably could not have been much more than the ABC of this bookkeeping. I therefore will not use its questionable title.

Interestingly, a similar sentiment was expressed much earlier by another German writer, Hager (1660). He too observed that, while it was true that double entry had come to Germany from Italy, the system was brought to perfection in the leading German cities after much effort and that it was not reasonable to call it the Italian system any longer.

The second reason is that the spirit of patriotism was greatly intensified in accounting circles after the publication of Jones's *English System* in 1796. This work was followed by other systems given national names. The supposed superiority of the Italian system of double entry was sometimes questioned. The turmoil may well have contributed to the diminishing use of the term "Italian" - even though double entry itself survived the assaults made upon it.

And with the decline in the use of the adjective "Italian", it appears that the use of Italian terms of art declined also. Growing pride in the national language may have contributed to this latter process. Wagner (1801) could note that the mischief of using foreign words "still persists in some measure, and has not been entirely rooted out; but the time is past, thank God, when the merchant was ashamed of his mother tongue". He repeated these sentiments in his new book published in the following year (1802). But he stated more clearly than before that the use of foreign words could not really be completely eliminated "because many terms or expressions are rather forced and ambiguous when expressed in German".

Postscript

On page 7 I refer to two German authors who claimed that the double-entry system should cease to be called the Italian system. Both authors were anticipated by a Dutchman, David Kock, who in his *Kort Onderricht van 't Italiaans Boekhouden,* 1650, wrote as follows: "But the enrichment of [the double-entry system] has occurred so notably and so abundantly here in this country, that one may say unreservedly that it is now not Italian, but Netherlandish or Dutch merchants bookeeeping" (quoted in K. Bes, *Bijdragen tot de Geschiedenis en de Thoerie van het Boekhouden*, 2nd.ed., Tilburg, 1908, p.146.)

References

Beckmann, J., *Beyträge zur Geschichte der Erfindungen*, Leipzig, 1783.

De Graaf, A., *Instructie van het Italiaans Boekhouden*, Hardewyk, 1693.

Flügel, G.T., *Theoretische Abhandlung vom doppelten Buchhalten*, Frankfurt, 1781.

Goessens, P., *Buchhalten fein kurtz zusammen gefasst*, Hamburg, 1594.

Hager, C.A., *Buchhalten...*,(?) Hamburg, 1660.

Hingstedt, C.E., *Die neuern praktischen Fortschritte im...Buchhalten*, Hamburg, 1804.

Jones, E.T., *English System of Book-keeping*, Bristol, 1796.

Kelly, P., *The Elements of Book-keeping*, London, 1801.

Maperger, P.J., *Probir-Stein derer Buch-Halter...*, Leipzig, 1718.

Mennher, V., *Practique brifue pour cyfrer et tenir Livres de Compte...*, Antwerp, 1550.

Pacioli, L., *Summa de Arithmetica...*, Venice, 1494.

Schreiber, H., *Ayn new kunstlich Buech...*, Vienna,(?) 1521.

Schweicker, W., *Zwifach Buchhalten...*, Nuremburg, 1549.

Stevin, S., *Vorstelicke Boeckhouding...*, Leiden, 1607.

Ten Have, O., *De Leer van het Boekhouden in de Nederlanden tijdens de Zeventiende en Achttiende Eeuw*, Delft, 1933.

Wagner, A., *Eduard T. Jones...Englische Buchhalterey...*, Leipzig, 1801.

_____ *Neues vollständiges...Lehrbuch...*, Magdeburg, 1802.

Weitnauer, A., *Venezianischer Handel der Fugger...*, Munich & Leipzig, 1931.

Ympyn, J., *Nieuwe Instructie ende Bewijs...*, Antwerp, 1543.

GEORGE PEACOCK, AN EARLY
'TRANSLATOR' OF PACIOLI

Like several other contemporary works of similar nature,
The Encyclopædia Metropolitana or Universal Dictionary of Knowledge,
published in London, 1817-1845, includes some material on bookkeeping
and accounts. It differs from others, however, in that the material
in the *Metropolitana* relates virtually exclusively to books on
bookkeeping, the lion's share being devoted to the exposition of
the double-entry system which forms part of Luca Pacioli's
Summa de arithmetica, Venice, 1494.[1]

The entry on bookkeeping appears in the historical part of
the lengthy chapter on Arithmetic in the first volume ("volume 1
[Pure Sciences, vol.1]") of the multi-volume work. This volume is
introduced by an Essay on Method by Samuel Taylor Coleridge, dated
January 1818. The chapter on arithmetic was written by George Peacock
(1791-1858), a distinguished Cambridge mathematician, Fellow of the
Royal Society and Bishop of Ely, a man of wide scholarly and
practical interests.[2]

---

1.   Pacioli is referred to as "Lucas de Burgo", the "de Burgo"
      being derived from his native Borgo San Sepolcro.

2.   *Dictionary of National Biography*, xliv, pp.138-40.

Peacock's account of Pacioli's treatment of bookkeeping
extends over seven of the thirteen paragraphs which make up the
discussion of bookkeeping. And these seven paragraphs concentrate
largely on the earlier chapters of Pacioli. Their contents are:
the "qualifications of a merchant, according to De Burgo" (para.226);
the inventory (para.227); the memorial (para.228); the journal
(para.229); the ledger (para.230); "modes of entering accounts of
different classes of transactions" (para.231); and miscellaneous
(para.232). The matter in paragraphs 226 to 230 is contained in
the first thirteen of Pacioli's 36 numbered and two unnumbered
chapters. Paragraphs 231 and 232 do no more than list some of the
topics covered in the remaining chapters.

It is evident that Peacock worked directly from Pacioli's
Summa, and not from Oldcastle's distinctly Paciolian *A profitable
treatyce*, London, 1543, known to us through Mellis's *A briefe
instruction*, London 1588.[3] Thus Peacock reproduces terms and
passages in Italian which are to be found in Pacioli but not
(in Italian) in Oldcastle. Further, his formulation of the introductory

---

3. Peacock mistakenly ascribed to "James Peele in 1569" the
re-publication "in an improved form" of Oldcastle's book,
with title the same as Mellis's title.

affirmation to precede an inventory of assets and liabilities is

a direct translation of Pacioli, whereas in Oldcastle there are

clear variations from it.[4] The sole pointer in the opposite direction

can be explained away readily. Pacioli writes in his chapter 4

that a merchant's head may be compared with one which has a hundred

eyes, and yet that these would not be enough for him. The

corresponding passage in Oldcastle runs: "...a marchant may be applied

unto Argus, which as Poetes shewe, had a hundreth eyes, so shoulde

a marchaunt be circumspect in his businesse". Peacock has the

following: "...if he [the merchant] possessed, like Argus, a hundred

eyes, they would not be sufficient". Peacock's rendering is far

closer to the sense of the original than Oldcastle's[5]; and the

mention of Argus, not named by Pacioli but evidently alluded to by

him, is easily accounted for as being a coincidence rather than a

derivation from Oldcastle by Peacock.

---

4.   Peacock departed only slightly from Pacioli. The year is
      1494, not 1493; and whereas Pacioli's formulation includes
      both alternatives, namely that the affirming merchant himself
      wrote the inventory or that he got someone else to write it
      ("...io de mia mano ho scripto overo fatto scrivere..."),
      Peacock takes the first only ("written with my own hand").
      Incidentally, he locates the merchant as "of the street of
      the Holy Apostle", whilst Pacioli has "de la contrada de
      Sancto Apostolo". Like most other translators and transcribers
      of Pacioli, the contracted word "contrada" in Pacioli was
      read as "strada", and so translated as "street". At the time
      there were no "strade" in Venice; and the reference is to
      the quarter or district named after the church of Santi
      Apostoli - it is odd that Pacioli used the singular form.

5.   The words "as Poetes shewe" in Oldcastle would seem to refer
      to a different idea expressed by Pacioli later in the same
      chapter.

Peacock did not simply paraphrase the various chapters
in Pacioli he selected for attention. Instead, he sometimes
re-arranged the material. For instance, his paragraph 226 quite
aptly merges material from Pacioli's chapter 4 with some from
chapter 1 - on the theme of the qualities and qualifications required
to be a good merchant. Again, he gives Pacioli's four designations
of the waste-book or memorial: memoriale, vacchetta and squartafoglio
from chapter 6, and squartafaccia from chapter 8 - the last three
rendered in English as "little cow, crooked leaf, or crooked face,
from its rumpled appearance when old". A further example concerns
the capital account. Capital, he explains in paragraph 229, "denotes
the whole stock in trade, (*monte e corpo di faculta o di tutto il
trafico*)". The words in Italian are an appropriate conflation of one
phrase in Pacioli's chapter 12 with another in chapter 5. Occasionally,
Peacock added something to the original. For example, he writes that
the ledger is the "last and more important book", whereas the title
of the corresponding chapter 13 in Pacioli refers to it only as the
"ultimo libro principale", the three account-books memorial, journal
and ledger being "li 3 libri principali" (title of chapter 5). And
in the discussion of the ruling of the ledger (para.230) Peacock
refers to columns "to contain the different denominations of money
or goods which were required to be registered", whilst Pacioli refers
only to money columns.

In one or two places Peacock plainly misunderstood the
original. One example concerns the balance in the cash account.
In chapter 12 Pacioli explains that the account must either have a

debit balance or be in balance (i.e. have a zero balance), but can never have a credit balance. It is rendered by Oldcastle as: "...for generally the Debitor syde must alwayes be more in summe of money than the Creditor syde of the chist [= chest, i.e. cash], or equall to the Creditor syde of the chyst, or els the balancing of your booke, or reckoning, there should fall and appeare an evident errour...". Peacock writes (para.229) that the cash account "in Italian book-keeping, properly so called, was never made *creditor*,... contrary to the usage of modern times".

Especially these last seven words suggest that Peacock had little real understanding of bookkeeping and accounting. His inadequate knowledge of the subject is revealed also in his precis of Pacioli's chapter 13. Peacock's paragraph 230 includes the following meaningless passage: "...the first page [of the ledger] contained the *cash* account; when *stock* was debtor, the general term *cavedale* was used; when creditor, the entry took place under the head of the particular goods which were concerned in the transaction...". It is not surprising that Peacock concentrated on those parts of the Pacioli text which required little knowledge of the finer points of double entry or little understanding of the system as a whole.

The last few paragraphs of Peacock refer to various books on bookkeeping after Pacioli, including one paragraph (234) on Simon Stevin, with acknowledgement to the German historian of inventions, Beckmann, as his source. The next and final paragraph mentions several eighteenth century works in English, concluding with a reference to Jones's system published in 1796, a system which was "essentially and unavoidably defective".

It has been assumed above that Peacock worked directly from Pacioli. It is possible, of course, that Peacock himself used an intermediate source, a now unknown published or unpublished work whose author had studied Pacioli at first hand. On this question, all that can be said usefully is that Peacock, as a mathematician, would have been aware of Pacioli's *Summa*. The inclusion of the paragraphs on Pacioli on bookkeeping may well have been due to Peacock's familiarity as mathematician with the famous *Summa*.

Peacock's account of Pacioli's work was used by Benjamin Franklin Foster in his *The Origins and Progress of Book-keeping*, London, 1852. The *Encyclopaedia Metropolitana* is specifically acknowledged as source. The borrowing is limited to material in Peacock's paragraphs 226, 227 and 228.

The material in Peacock re-appears again in William Murray, *Historical sketch of the Science of Accountantship, and the rise and progress of the art, from the earliest period to the present time; compiled from various sources;...*, London, 1862. (Professor L. Goldberg drew my attention to this publication). Murray, however, did not acknowledge his source specifically, though he took far more from the encyclopaedia than did Foster - in fact, he reproduced, with only minor modifications in most cases, material from all of Peacock's paragraphs except the last. There can be no doubt whatever that Murray worked directly from Peacock as regards the material on Pacioli.

In only three minor matters is there some difference.
Referring to Lucas de Burgo, he writes: "Sancti Sepulchri as he
has been termed..." (p.16). This latter designation of Pacioli
is not to be found in Peacock. The form "Luce de Burgo sancti
Sepulchri "appears in Pacioli's *Summa*. This suggests that Murray
had seen the *Summa*, or a reference to the *Summa* other than in
Peacock. Murray also states that Pacioli's work is "the earliest
known work on the subject of bookkeeping" - a point made in Foster,
in different words, but not in Peacock. Finally, Murray writes
that Pacioli, "without knowing much of trade by his own experience",
"observed the manner in which intelligent merchants of his country
kept their accounts" (p.15). This observation does not appear in
either Peacock or Foster.

Murray also made use of the material in Peacock's paragraphs
233 and 234 which deal with authors other than Pacioli. Here
Murray added some further information. And the rest of his small
book gives a good deal of information about various authors and
books which is not to be found in Peacock.

TWO TYPOGRAPHICAL AMBIGUITIES
IN PACIOLI'S 'SUMMA':
FURTHER NOTES

BASIL S. YAMEY

TWO TYPOGRAPHICAL AMBIGUITIES IN
PACIOLI'S ›SUMMA‹: FURTHER NOTES

In the Gutenberg-Jahrbuch of 1976 (pp. 156–161) I examined two typographical ambiguities which appear in Distinctio IX, Tractatus XI, ›Particularis de Computis et Scripturis‹, of Luca Pacioli's ›Summa di Arithmetica, Geometria, Proportioni et Proportionalita‹, Venice, 1494. Further information is presented here about these ambiguities, which in each case concerns the illustration in the book of two parallel oblique strokes or lines.

I

The first practice, discussed in sections 1 to 3 of the original paper, relates to the two slanting lines or strokes used in the early Venetian form of the double-entry journal to mark off the debit part of an entry from the credit. The information given in the original paper offers no explanation why *two* lines were used rather than merely one.

In fact, Domenico Manzoni (from whose ›Quaderno doppio‹, Venice, Comin di Tridino, 1540, I drew both a quotation and an illustration), did provide an explanation, which I failed to notice. This explanation is that the two slanting lines signify that from each entry in the journal two entries have always to be made in the ledger:

... lequali dinotano, che d'una partida del giornale, sempre se ne convien far due nel quaderno.

Simon Grisogono, in his ›Il mercante arrichito del perfetto quaderniere ...‹. Venice, Alessandro Vechhi, 1609, provided the same explanation or rationalisation:

... due lineete a traverso // lequali separa il debitore dal creditore significando che d'una partida che scrivi nel giornale n'hai da far due nel quaderno ...

This explanation was repeated a year later in Giovanni Antonio Moschetti: Dell' universal trattato di libri doppii. Venice: Luca Valentini, 1610 (misprinted as MDCXC), although Moschetti idiosyncratically used two horizontal strokes (=) instead of two sloping strokes:

Fatta la partida in Giornale nè devi portar due in Libro [= ledger] cioè una in dar, l'altra in haver, che questo significano le due lineete di Giornale = ...

The explanation appears again in Ludovico Flori's ›Trattato del modo di tenere il libro doppio domestico ...‹, Palermo, Decio Cirillo, 1636[1]. A side-heading asks the question: »Che cosa siano, & a che servino quelle due lineette //.« The answer in the text is:

Quelle due lineette poi // nō servono per altro se non per distinguere il Debitore dal Creditore: E per accennare, che d'ogni partita scritta nel Giornale se ne devono far due a Libro, cioè una in debito al conto del Debitore, & una in credito al conto del Creditore[2].

Manzoni, Grisogono, Moschetti and Flori all dealt with journal entries in the Venetian style. It is interesting to find this style mentioned in a book published in Danzig in 1592: Wolffgang Sartorius: Buchhalten mit zwey Büchern ... – This book

---

1 In his preface, Flori refers to Pacioli, Grisogono and Moschetti, among others.

2 In my earlier paper (p. 158) I quote another passage from Flori, where, however, no explanation is offered.

begins with a brief exposition in verse of rules for bookkeeping[3].

Den Schuldner lern erkennen wohl
An den Wörtlein/Für/und/sol/
Den Creditor man kennen kan
An den Wörtlein/sol haben/und an.
Setz zur Lincken Hand den Schuldner
Und zur Rechten den Gleubiger,
Unterscheid sie mit zwey strichlein
Welche also // gezeichnet sein ...

The words ›für‹ and ›an‹ take the place of the Italian ›per‹ and ›a‹.

II

The explanation given by Manzoni and others of the two oblique lines corresponds with that given by Pacioli of the two oblique lines drawn across a journal entry to cancel it – the subject of sections 4 and 5 of my original paper. For these two cancellation lines signify to the bookkeeper that the information in the journal entry has been entered twice into the ledger, once to the debit of one account, and once to the credit of another.

Moschetti repeats the instruction given by Pacioli. When the debit has been posted to the ledger, one must give the journal entry »il primo taglio cominciando dal principio della righa nel fondo della partita, & ascendendo verso man destra ...«; when the credit has been posted, ›il secondo taglio‹ is to be made (libro primo, cap. 10). The two illustrative journals do not have these cancellation lines.

After the first journal, however, an explanation of the omission is given in an ›Avvertimento al lettore‹. The lines should have been there, according to the rules, but were left out to ease the task of the printer; and the reader's intellect will visualise what his corporal eye does not see:

> Attendi con accuratezza Lettor Carissimo che quantunque nelle precedenti Partite ... tu non veda i tagli che fare di necessità vi si devono, mentre nel Maestro [= ledger] suo sono trasferite, li quali conforme alle regole del Primo Libro, in questa maniera hanno ad attraversare ciascheduna Partita

> non è però onde tu gli debba da esse Partite escludere anzi che dove à tralasciarli la commodità dello Stampatore ci hà persuaso, la tua Prudenza nondimeno tale esser deve che ciò, che l'occhio corporal non vede, l'intelletto, che è spirituale conosca, & dove manca la stampa rimembranza dell sour'accennate regole supplisca.

3 I have not been able to examine a copy of this rare work. I have followed the spelling and punctuation as in *B. Penndorf:* Geschichte der Buchhaltung in Deutschland. Leipzig 1913, p. 147.

364

ADDENDA

SOME REFLECTIONS ON THE WRITING OF A

GENERAL HISTORY OF ACCOUNTING

On page 135, I discuss Michael Baxandall's views on the
reception of Italianate ideas and people in South Germany at the
beginning of the sixteenth century. I have inadvertently mis-
represented the author. The key sentences are: "Italian art went
with these and many other.Italian things and was not an isolated
artistic exotic... The city's new men had use for both Italianate
ideas and Italianate people of various kinds". Schwarz, the head
bookkeeper of the Fugger, is then considered as one example among
several.

My comments on Baxandall's observations on Schwarz and
his manuscript nevertheless are applicable.

OLDCASTLE, PEELE AND MELLIS

Mellis's magpie tendencies are evident in the illustrative set of account-books he added to the (modified) Oldcastle text. A few of his borrowings have already been noted. Further examples follow here.

As shown elsewhere, the entry in Mellis's inventory for "lands and rents, within the countie of Norf" is based on a lengthy entry in the inventory in Weddington's *A Breffe Instruction*, 1567.[1] A second entry for lands and rents is also based on Weddington. (For convenience, all roman numerals in the originals are expressed here in arabic numerals. A standard form has been adopted for money amounts.)

(W)   More in Andwarpe one dwellinge house namid the
        crowne standinge in the long new stret within the
        perrishe of oure lady, pourchasid to me and my eyres
        for ever of one M.W. after 16. yeres pourchase, the
        yerly rent wherof is £20. - fls. as by the writtingis
        therof more plainly aperethe datid the 25. daie of
        Marche last Anno 1559. the wiche cost me in redy
        money £320. - fls. the wiche I do now exsteme at
        £340. - fls. ...

———

1.   B.S. Yamey, "John Weddington's *A Breffe Instruction*, 1567",
        Accounting Research, vol.9, 1958; reprinted in my
        Essays on the History of Accounting, Arno Press, New York,
        1978. Some other examples are also given in that article.

(M)   Item, more here in London mine own dwelling
house in saint Clements lane, purchased to
me and my heires for ever, of one W.J. after
16.yeres purchase, the yerelie rent whereof is
£10. as by the writings thereof more plainly
appeareth. Dated the 25. day of March, An.1581.
The which cost me in redy money £230. the which
I doe now esteeme at £280...

Mellis took more from Weddington's inventory. Here are
some examples.

(W)   More in householde Stuff of divers sortis to saie -
In my bedchamber one bedstede of ioyners worke
the wiche I do exsteme to be worthe £10.13.4.
More one fether bed, and one bolster worthe £6.10.-.
More there in a whit chest divers sortis of
lynnen as shettis pellow berres shortis
napkins &c. all worthe £20.-.-.
Somma in all withe in my chamber amonteth £37.3.4.

(M)   Item, more in housholde stuffe of divers sortes, to say.
In my bed chamber one bedsted of Joyners worke,
which I doe esteeme worth £10.8.4.
More one fetherbed and bolster, worth £6.10.
More there in a white chest, diverse sortes
of linnen, vz. twenty five paire of sheetes,
thirty pillowberes, twenty shirtes, and sixe
dosen table napkins. All together I esteeme at £20.
Summe in all the said chamber amounteth to £37.03.04.

(W)   More in marchandize of divers sortis within
        my house to saie -
        In my pachouse western Carsais peaces 100. of
        divers collors to saie blewz peaces 30. waggettis
        peaces 60. reddis peaces 6. light grens
        peaces 4. In all peaces 100. content 17½ yardis
        the peace one with a nother at 49s.
        the peace amontethe £249.-.-.
        More sais of Arras peaces 11. to saie 4. peaces
        blacke at 36s the peace £7.4.-.
        Incarnations peaces 4. at 40s. the peace
        amontethe £8.-.-.
        Reddis peaces 3. at 44s. the peace amontethe
        £6.12.-.
        In all for the says as afore saide amontethe £20.16.-.

(M)   Item more in Marchandise of divers sorts within
        my house, to say:
        In my packhouse westerne carsies peeces 100. of
        divers colours, to say, blewes, peeces 30.
        watcheds peeces 60. reddes peeces 6. light
        greenes peeces 4. all which cost one with
        another, 59s. the peece, which hundred
        peeces amount in all to the summe of £245.00.00.
        More sayes of arras, peeces 11. to say ,
        4. peeces black at 36s. the peece amounteth
        to £7.4s.
        More in carnation peeces, 4. at 40s. the peece,
        amount to £8.
        More reddes peeces 3. at 44s. per peece,
        amounteth to £6.12s.
        All which said sayes amount to £21.16.00.

        Mellis appropriated even more material from James Peele's

book, *The Pathe waye to perfectnes...*,1569. The borrowings are

both from the "private" account-books in Peele, referred to here

as PP, and from other sets of books, the business books (for the

"trafique in marchaundies"), referred to here as PB. Some examples

follow.

In the name of God. Amen
                            1566
                    December the 31 daye.

The Inventorie generall of me Frauncis Twyforde
Cittezin and Mercer of London dwellinge
in the parishe of saint Swithens contayninge
my whole estate in Landes, Rentes, Goodes,
ready monie Debtes and Creditours aswell
in my own custody and also in Trafique of
Marchaundies in thorder of my servaunte
Anthonie Rice...

In the name of God Amen.
                            1587
                    August the 8 day.

The Inventorie generall of me N.A.
Citizen and N. of London, dwelling in
the parish of S. Swithins, Contayning
my whole estate generall in lands, rents,
goods, readie money, debtes, and Creditors
which I have in this world at this
present day.

                         . . . . .

[In the list of gold coins in the inventory]

(PP)   20 Portigues at £3.10. per pece £70.

(M)   64 Portigues at £3.10. the peece £224.

                         . . . . .

[In the list of plate in the inventory]

(PP)   Thirdlye in Sylver Plate all whyte, that is to saye.
        - 2 Nestes of Boules withe covers all poiz
        7 unces 1 gr.
        - 3 Haunse pottes of pyntes a pece for Beare
        all wayinge...

(M)   Secondly, in silver plate all white,
                    two nestes of boules with covers, all
                    wayinge 36 oz.
        Two haunse pottes of pints for beere, all
                    waying 16 oz.

. . . . .

[The conclusion of the inventory]

(PP)   To con-
           clude this   The Generall Charge.   £11941.13.01.
           Inventorie   The Generall Discharge   £00018.13.04.
           I finde   My stocke or net substaunce £11922.19.09.

                                                              R.

(M)   To con-
           clude, in   The general charge   £2483 00 06
           this said   The generall discharge   0193 17 06
           Inventory I   For my stock, or net substance 2289 03 00
           find.

                                                              R.

. . . . .

[In the inventory, one of the debts]

(PB)   Item, Bartram Banckes, Cittizen and
        Vintener of London, owethe by an
        Obligacion payable the 8 daye of Februarye
        nexte, for readye monie lent him. £153.12.6.

(M)   Item William Hall Citizen and Vintner
        of London, oweth me by an obligation payable
        at Michaelmas next comming, for redy money
        lent him, £153.12.6.

. . . . .

[One of the creditors]

(PB)   Item. There is owinge to Thomas Brampton of
Bristowle Marchaunte for the rest of an
accompte, betwene him and my Master for
a partable voyage into Spayne...dewe at
his pleasure for the somme of. £53.17.6

(M)   Item. I owe unto Thomas Barton of Bristow
Marchant, for the rest of an accompt betweene
him and me for a partable viage into
Spaine, due at his pleasure, the somme of
£53.17.06.

· · · · ·

[An item of merchandise]

(PB)   Item. Cyvill Oylles 9 tonnes in 18 pypes
now remayninge whiche is vallewed at
£20 the tonne amounte to. £180.

(M)   Item Civil oyles 12. tunnes in 24. pipes
now remayning, which is valued at £20
the tunne, amounts to £240.

· · · · ·

[A journal entry]

(PB)   Expences of housolde oweth, To mony. £16.6.3.
and is for so much paide oute since the seconde
daye of Januarye last past, aswell for meate
and drinke as also for apparel and such other
like charges, as by the perticulers in the
booke entituled expences of housolde.

(M)   Expences of householde oweth to money £10.3.0.
            And is for so much payde out since the 8 of
            August last past. As wel for meat & drink,
            as also for apparrel, and such other charges,
            as by the particulers in ye booke entituled
            Expences of houshold

· · · · ·

[Opening credit entry in capital account in ledger]

(PP)   Stocke generall being the substaunce of my
            Fraunces Twiforde Citezin and Mercer of London
            at this present is dewe to have £11922.19.09.
            and is the very net rest proceaded of
            mine Inventorye generall all and all manner
            of my Creditours deducted (the increase
            wherof God grant if it be his will)...

(M)   Stock generall being the substance of me N.A.
            Citizen and N. of London, at this present is
            due to have £2289.03. And is the very net rest
            proceeded of mine inventorie generall, al & al
            manner of my creditors deducted... The increase
            wherof God grant if it be his will. Amen.

COMPOUND JOURNAL ENTRIES

1.   Two further examples in the early literature of the use
of compound journal entries: (a) According to de Waal, they are
used in Claesz Pietersz, *Boeckhouwen op die Italiaensche Maniere...*,
1595. I have not been able to examine a copy of the book.
(b) Compound entries appear frequently in the illustrative journal
in Jan Coutereels, *Den Stijl van Boeck-houden*, Middelburg, 1603.
There are noughts in the posting columns for the collective debits
or credits. These are referred to as "sundry accounts" "sundry
merchandise" or "sundry persons", according to the context.
Coutereels' book was published presumably after Stevin's text had
been written, but before the latter was published.

2.   The example of a ledger-posting reference from Weddington's
book, given on page 324, appears without the second "31" in the
original. However, the corresponding entries in ledger accounts
would not balance without it. The details can be arranged in
this way:

Peper drie...for the accompte of Johan Ede	31	£114.17.4	
Ede...his accompt corrant	38	53.15.1	
Ede...his accompt of tyme	42	61. 2.3	
Accompt in mount	21		£112.11.6
Chargis of marchandize	17		1.1
Provizion	28		2. 4.9
Peper drie...for...Ede	31		114.17.4

"Provizion" is "commission". The "accompt in mount" is explained in the article, "The 'Partimenti' Account", reprinted in this volume.

THE INDEX TO THE LEDGER

1.　　　　Information about the ledger indexes in a surviving collection
of early Medici account-books is given by Florence Edler [de Roover]
in her *Glossary*. Each ledger may have had its *stratto*. Each
surviving *stratto* is a separate book, and is usually half the width
of the corresponding ledger, but of the same length. The indexes
have "thumb-initials like a modern dictionary, except that they are
usually very artistic in design and colored or illuminated". The
index had its normal place "between the front cover and the title-
page" of its ledger. Few of the surviving examples are labelled in
any way, contrary to the directions given in early treatises. The
stratti are not arranged as double indexes. An account is listed
on the appropriate page according to its first word: the Christian
name for personal accounts; and the first word (even if it is the
definite or indefinite article) for other accounts. (Florence Edler,
Glossary of Mediaeval Terms of Business, Italain Series 1200-1600,
Cambridge, Mass., 1934, p.370.

2.　　　　The Banco di Bilbao in 1980 published a facsimile edition
of the "Libro Mayor" (1498-1500) of Ochoa Perez de Salinas,
"banquero" at the Spanish royal court. The ABCDARIO" (index) is a
separate slim booklet. In height it is slightly smaller than the
ledger it accompanies; and its width is about half that of the
ledger. The alphabetic staircase is unusual. It begins at the

left-hand corner of the top of the booklet, proceeding to the letter H at the right-hand top corner. The letters then proceed downwards. S is the last letter to have its step. The compiler must have run out of patience. The entries to T, V and X are made on the reverse side of the page allocated to S, without any further ado.

3.   Some of the early ledgers preserved in the archives of the Banco di Napoli, Naples, have complicated index books. Each of the indexes in question is sub-divided into four sections. Each section has its own alphabetic staircase; the pages are cut so that all four staircases are visible together. The first three sections are allocated to clients with Christian names beginning with A, F and G respectively. The fourth section is for the remaining clients. A client "Francesco Pagano" would be entered in the second section on the page for P, i.e. surnames beginning with P. (*L'Archivio Storico del Banco di Napoli*, Naples, 1972, p.85. This page illustrates the *pandetta* of the creditors' ledger of the Banco del Popolo, for the second half of 1795.)

4.   Space saving in the preparation of early treatises is evident in James Peele's *Pathe waye to perfectnes...*, London, 1569. Three ledgers are included in the specimen account-books. One index suffices for all three ledgers. Each page is divided horizontally into three sections, one for each ledger. A note explains that this has been done "to thintent to save the making of three kallenders,

which wold encrease the largenes of this printed Boke".   "Yet

in bookes of effecte, every greate boke requirethe his kallender".